Indian Classical Literature: A Brief Synopsis

"Indian Classical Literature: A Brief Synopsis" is an initiative to help BA level students to understand the Indian classical literature. This book deals with the aspects of classical literature in the easiest way making it convenient for the BA level students to understand it at ease. Keeping in mind the CBCS course, each chapter deals with the units descriptively.

About the Author

Deepali Borthakur, MA, MSW, M.Phil., Assistant Professor, English Faculty of Commerce, Management, Humanities and Social Sciences, Assam down town University.

INDIAN CLASSICAL LITERATURE
A Brief Synopsis

Deepali Borthakur

CONCEPT PUBLISHING COMPANY PVT. LTD.
NEW DELHI-110059

Indian Classical Literature: A Brief Synopsis written by **Deepali Borthakur**, M.A, MSW, M.Phil., Assistant Professor, English Faculty of Commerce, Management, Humanities and Social Science, Assam down town University, Guwahati, is an initiative to help BA level students to understand the Indian classical literature. This book deals with the aspects of classical literature in the easiest way making it convenient for the BA level students to understand it at ease. Keeping in mind the CBCS course, each chapter deals with the units descriptively.

BOOK CODE - ENG. - 4

ISBN-13: 978-93-88937-21-4 (HB)

ISBN-13: 978-93-88937-22-1 (PB)

First Published 2019

Published and Printed by

Concept
Since 1974

Concept Publishing Company Pvt. Ltd.
A/15-16, Commercial Block, Mohan Garden
New Delhi-110059 (INDIA)
Phones : 91 11 25351460, 91 11 25351794
Email : publishing@conceptpub.com;
Website : www.conceptpub.com

Preface

"Indian Classical Literature: A Brief Synopsis" represents an attempt, if only a crude one, to broaden the prospect of the literature aspirants. Belonging to the specialization of Indian writing in English, Indian Classical Literature always fascinated me. Indian Classical literature is the root that has bestowed Indian literature glory and significance in the present scenario. Indian literature cannot subsist without following the footprints of the classics. Contemporary playwright Girish Karnad has taken classics as the base of his dramas like Yayati, Naga-Mandala, Hayavadana, Tughla etc.

As we Know that literature is the reflection of our society and as such classical literature holds an important position. It makes us familiar with our old traditions, mythology, beliefs and social system.

Indian Classical Literature holds classics like *The Mahabharatha*. The classics are forever that though they are supposed to have happened a long time back, we can relate them to the present-day aspects.

We can compare the classics of Indian Literature with present day or in the future to analyze or understand what is happening actually. We can also argue on that point that the world is changing and how we can still hold on to ancient literature. We can see that situations are same though everything else is changing. It's very important to hold on to our traditions; culture as these factors makes us what we are. These factors give us our identity. Therefore it is very important to know about classical literature that forms the background of our existence.

Indian Classics are important to analyze the world irrespective of the time we live in. It can always help us in some way or other to deal with things or to understand this world better.

This book will give an insight into the concept of Classical Literature, keeping in view the undergraduate syllabus and students. The first chapter starts with the definition and introduction of classical literature followed by four chapters that deal with the various units as declared in the CBCS syllabus. The book discusses masterpieces such as Vyasa's *The Mahabharata* Kalidasa's *Abhijnanashakuntalam* and *Mrichchakatikam* and how these texts aimed not at persuasion but ecstasy or lifting the reader out of himself. This book also focuses on the masterpieces of Assamese Classical Literature. Shankardeva and his dramas that hold an important position as a part of Assamese and world literature have occupied a chapter in this book.

I believe, "Indian Classical Literature: A Brief Synopsis" will be helpful for the students pursuing their graduation and also to literature aspirants who have a keen interest in Indian Classical Literature.

Acknowledgement

At the foremost, I would like to express my sincere gratitude towards Dr. Mridul Bordoloi, The Head of Department, Department of English, Dibrugarh University for invaluable guidance and support. It would not have been possible for me to complete my book without his motivational and scholarly supervision.

I am immensely indebted to and extend my sincere gratitude to my PhD Supervisor Dr. Basil N. Darlong Diengdoh, Assistant Professor, Dibrugarh University who has been extremely kind to extend his scholarly insights that helped me accomplish the work.

The completion of this book would have been a dream without the care, concern of my family members and friends especially Tinku Das. I extend my heartiest gratitude to my loving parents for their care, patience and continuous support and for bearing with me in my difficult moments during the pursuance of this book.

At the end, I would like to thank Almighty whose blessings always helped me to move forward in life.

DETAILED SYLLABUS

B.A. (Hons.) English under CBCS
DIBRUGARH UNIVERSITY-2018
First Semester

Core Course: 10100
Course 1: Indian Classical Literature
(Core)

CREDITS ASSIGNED: 6 CREDITS

UNIT 1: CLASSICAL SANSKRIT DRAMA
Kalidasa, *Abhijnana Shakuntalam*, tr. Chandra Rajan, in *Kalidasa: The Loom of Time* (New Delhi: Penguin, 1989).

UNIT II: SELECTIONS FROM EPIC SANSKRIT LITERATURE
Vyasa, "The Dicing and The Sequel to Dicing", "The Book of the Assembly Hall", "The Temptation of Karna", Book V "The Book of Effort" in *The Mahabharata*: tr. and ed. J.A.B. van Buitenen (Chicago: Brill, 1975) pp. 106-69.

UNIT III: SANSKRIT DRAMA
Sudraka, *Mrcchakatika*, tr. M.M. Ramachandra Kale (New Delhi: Motilal Banarasidass, 1962).

UNIT IV: CLASSICAL ASSAMESE DRAMA
Shankaradeva, *Parijata Harana* [trans. William L. Smith] from *Krishna. A Source Book*, ed. Edwin Francis Bryant (London: OUP, 2007). [www.atributetosankaradeva.org/parijata.pdf]

DETAILED SYLLABUS

B.A. (Hons.) English under CBCS
DELHI UNIVERSITY

Core Course
Paper 1: Indian Classical Literature

Unit I. Kalidasa *Abhijnana Shakuntalam*, tr. Chandra Rajan, in Kalidasa: The Loom of Time (New Delhi: Penguin, 1989).

Unit II. Vyasa 'The Dicing' and 'The Sequel to Dicing, 'The Book of the Assembly Hall', 'The Temptation of Karna', Book V 'The Book of Effort', in The Mahabharata: tr. and ed. J.A.B. van Buitenen (Chicago: Brill, 1975) pp.106–69.

Unit III. Sudraka *Mrcchakatika*, tr. M.M. Ramachandra Kale (New Delhi: Motilal Banarasidass, 1962).

Unit IV. Ilango Adigal 'The Book of Banci', in Cilappatikaram: The Tale of an Anklet, tr. R. Parthasarathy (Delhi: Penguin, 2004) book 3.

Contents

1
Classical Sanskrit Drama

Indian Literature is one of the oldest and richest literatures around the world. The Indian Constitution recognizes 22 official languages. Each language has its regional literature. Indian drama and theatre has the longest and richest tradition in theatres across the world. Sanskrit- is the primary sacred language of Hinduism, a philosophical language in Buddhism, Hinduism and Jainism.

Bharata is considered the founder of the Indian dramaturgy and he described drama as the "fifth Veda." His *Natyasastra* in Sanskrit appears to be the first attempt to develop and arrange the technique or rather art of drama in a systematic manner. Bharata says in *Natyasastra:* "The drama as I have devised will give courage, amusement and happiness as well as counsel to them all" (111-112).

The earliest form of Indian drama which is Sanskrit drama began after the development of Greek and Roman drama and before the development of theatre in other parts of Asia. It emerged sometime between the 2nd century B.C. and the 1st century B.C. and flourished between the 1st century and the 10th century, which was a period of relative peace in the history of India during which hundreds of plays were written. With the Islamic conquests that began in the 10th and 11th centuries, theatre was discouraged or forbidden entirely. Later, in an attempt to re-assert indigenous values and ideas, village theatre was encouraged across the subcontinent, developing in a large number of regional languages from the 15th to the 19th centuries. Modern Indian theatre developed during the period of colonial rule under the British Empire, from the mid-19th century until the mid-20th. The earliest-surviving fragments of Sanskrit drama date from the 1st century. The wealth of archeological evidence from earlier periods offers no indication of the existence of a tradition of theatre. The ancient *Vedas* (hymns from between 1500 to 1000 B.C. that are among the earliest examples of literature in the world) contain no hint of it (although a small number are composed in a form of dialogue) and the rituals of the Vedic period do not appear to have developed into theatre. The *Mahābhāṣya* by Patañjali contains the earliest reference to what may have been the seeds of Sanskrit drama. This treatise on grammar from 140 B.C. provides a feasible date for the beginnings of theatre in India. Overall, Sanskrit drama was the main source of Indian theatre with culture, customs and ethnicity.

There are references regarding drama in Patanjali's 'Vyakarna', Vatsyana's 'Kamsutra', Kautilya's 'Arthashastra' and Panini's 'Ashtabhyam'. Therefore the origin of Sanskrit drama dates back to 2000 B.C. It is clear that the Hindus of over 2000 years ago had their own theory of drama and that their dramatic practice avoided both the severe austerity of Greek tragedy and opulent extravagance of the ancient Chinese drama. But it is very difficult to trace the origin of the Indian theatre with exact date of its commencement. Even though there are contradictory opinions about origin of Indian theatre among scholar, but all this shows that classical Sanskrit drama probably originated from the folk theatre of the country. Whatever the origin of the classical drama on the one hand, we have playwrights like Kalidasa, Bhavbhuti, Sudraka, Harsha and Vishakadatta; on the other hand we have the exponents of dramatic art like Bharata, Bhatta, Abhinavagupta, Dhananjaya, Ramchandra and Ashvaghosha etc. All these are the pioneers of classical Sanskrit drama in India.

Elements of Sanskrit Drama

All literature in Sanskrit is classified into Drishya (that can be seen or exhibited) and the Shravya (that can be heard or recited). While poetry in all forms can be said to fall under Shravya category; and drama comes under the Drishya form. Drama in Sanskrit literature is covered under the broad umbrella of 'Rupaka' which means depiction of life in its various aspects represented in forms by actors who assume various roles. A rupaka has ten classifications of which 'Nataka' (drama), the most important one, has come to mean all dramatic presentations. The Sanskrit drama grows around three primary constituents namely Vastu (plot), Neta (hero), and Rasa (sentiment). The plot could be either principal (adhikarika), or accessory (prasangika). The former concerns the primary characters of the theme and pervades the entire play. The later serves to the further and supplement the main topic and relates to subordinate characters other than the chief ones. The Neta (hero), according to the definition prescribed by Natyashashtra, is always depicted as modest (vineeta), sweet tempered (madhura), sacrificing (tyagi), capable (daksha), civil in talk (priyamvada), belonging to noble family (taptaloka), pure (suchi), articulate (vagmi), consistent (sthera), young (yuva), endowed with intellect (buddhi), enthusiasm (utsaha), good memory (smrthi), strong (dridha), energetic (tejaswi), learned (pandita) and pious (dharmic). Overall, the hero in sanskrit drama falls in the category of 'Dheerodatta' which means a hero who is brave and sublime at any time in every situation.

Major Sanskrit Playwrights

Bharata: Sage Bharata was an ancient Indian musicologist and worldwide popular as an author of **'Natya Shastra'**, a theoretical treatise on ancient Indian dramaturgy and histrionics dated between roughly 400 B.C. and 200 B.C. There is a legend regarding Sage Bharata and his treatise 'Natya Shastra' that when Gods asked Brahma to create a Veda that could be understood by commoners, sothat Brahma created the 'Panchamaveda' (fifth veda) called 'Natya Veda'. Drawing pathya (words) from the Rig Veda, abhinaya (gesture) from the Yajurveda, geet (music) from Samaveda and rasa (sentiment and emotion) from Atharvaveda, he synthesized Natya Veda. After creating Natya Veda, Brahma asked sage Bharata to popularize it on earth. Thus 'Natya Shastra' came into existence as a concrete foundation of Indian drama tradition

Bharata composed 'Natya Shastra' approximately in the third century, originally written in Sanskrit consisting 6000 sutras or verse stanzas incorporated in 36 chapters. The title can be loosely translated as 'A Compendium of theatre or a manual of Dramatic art'. The 'Natya Shastra' legend indicates an intimate relation between the idea of dancing and dramatic representation. According to Bharata, poetry, dance and mime in life's play produce emotion but only drama produces flavor (Rasa). The drama uses the eight basic emotions of love, joy, anger, sadness, pride, fear, aversion, and wonder attempting to resolve them in the ninth holistic feeling of peace. Thus, when the dramatic art was well comprehended, the 'Natya Veda' was performed on the occasion of the celebration of Lord Indra's victory over the 'Assuras' and 'Danavas'. In the 'Natya Shastra', there is a verse in its sixth chapter which can be quoted as Bharat Muni's own summary of his dramatic theory-

> "The combination called Natya is a mixture of rasa, bhavas, abhinayas, Dharmis, varttis, pravrittis, siddhi, svaras, instrument, song and theatre House."

Bharata, the great author prescribes not only the stage worthy things which are both entertaining and didactic but also the qualifications for the audience. His 'Natya Shastra' highlights almost all aspects of drama- stage setting, music, plot construction, characterization, dialogue and acting. 'Rasa' is another significant gift given to the Indian classical theatre by Bharata. Even in contemporary India the term 'rasa' means 'flavour' is used colloquially (local language) to describe the aesthetic experience. There are eight basic rasas proposed by Bharata such as- love, joy (humour), anger, sadness, pride, fear, aversion, and wonder. These all eight basic rasas attempt to resolve in the ninth holistic rasa of peace. These nine rasas are co-related with bhavas, the imitation of emotions that actors perform. Many scholars tried their hand in comparing Aristotle with Sage Bharata. Their study reveals that the western theory of drama derives from Aristotle's '**Poetics**'. His theory of drama can more properly be called the theory of tragedy, peculiarly, a Greek concept. On the other hand, Bharata's conception of drama is based on the Indian theory of 'Karma'. According to this theory, man is not just the play thing in the hands of fate but the architect of his own destiny. His fate is determined by his own actions. Obviously there is a fundamental difference between Aristotle and Sage Bharata, which determines the different approach to drama, which is western and Indian. Nevertheless, Sanskrit drama, in its long and checkered history, has throughout conformed to these classical norms prescribed by Bharata in his famous treatise 'Natya Shastra'. The best Sanskrit drama had been intimately associated with stir and manifoldness of the life of a cultured class of people like Sage Bharata. The same tradition continued by other prominent scholars such as- Bhasa, Shudraka, Kalidasa, Harsha, Bhavbhuti and Vishakadutta and their creative Sanskrit works are the product of vigorous creative energy as well as sustained technical excellence.

Bhasa: Another prominent Sanskrit playwright was Bhasa, who is the oldest known dramatist, might have flourished some time between 500 B.C. to 50 B.C. a period certainly earlier than that of a celebrated grammarian Panini. Thirty-five plays are to be said written by him, but only thirteen plays are in record at present. Bhāsa does not follow all the dictates of the Natya Shastra. This has been taken as a proof of their antiquity; no post-Kālidāsan play has been found to break the rules of the 'Natya Shastra'. Bhāsa allows scenes that contain signs of physical violence to be shown on stage in plays like Urubhanga. This is strictly frowned upon by Natya Shastra. The ***Uru-Bhanga*** and ***Karna-bhara*** are the only known tragic Sanskrit plays in ancient India. Though branded the villain of the *Mahabharata*, Duryodhana is the actual hero in *Uru-Bhanga* shown repenting his past as he lies with his thighs crushed awaiting death. His relations with his family are shown with great pathos. The epic contains no reference to such repentance. The *Karna-bhara* ends with the premonitions of the sad end of Karna, another epic character from *Mahabharata*. Early plays in India, inspired by Natya Shastra, strictly considered sad endings inappropriate. The plays are generally short compared to later playwrights and most of them draw the theme from the Indian epics, ***Mahabharata*** and ***Ramayana.*** Though he is firmly on the side of the heroes of the epic, Bhāsa treats their opponents with great sympathy. He takes a lot of liberties with the story to achieve this. In the ***Pratima-nataka***, Kaikeyi who is responsible for the tragic events in the Ramayana is shown as enduring the calumny of all so that a far noble end is achieved.

Kalidasa: Kālidāsa was a renowned Classical Sanskrit writer, widely regarded as the greatest poet and dramatist in the Sanskrit language. Nothing apart from his works is known with certainty about the life of Kālidāsa, such as his period or where he lived. Little is known about Kālidāsa's life. There has been great ambiguity regarding the exact date of Kālidāsa but in 1986, Sanskrit scholar Ramchandra Tiwari of Bhopal claims to have conducted a thorough research on Kalidasa and after analysing 627 archaeological evidences which included 104 sculptures, 30 pictures and 493 scriptural words determined that Kalidasa lived in the period 370-450AD. Kālidāsa wrote three plays. Among them, '**Abhijñānaśākuntalam**' generally regarded as a masterpiece. It was among the first Sanskrit works to be translated into English which is the story of King Dushyanta who, while on a hunting trip, meets Shakuntalā, the adopted daughter of a sage, and marries her. A mishap befalls them when he is summoned back to court: Sakuntala, pregnant with their child, inadvertently offends a visiting sage and incurs a curse, by which Dushyanta will forget her completely until he sees the ring he has left with her. On her trip to Dushyanta's court in an advanced state of pregnancy, she loses the ring, and has to come away unrecognized. The ring is found by a fisherman who recognizes the royal seal and returns it to Dushyanta, who regains his memory of Sakuntala and sets out to find her. After more travels, they are finally reunited.

Another important work '**Vikramorvasivam**' ("Pertaining to Vikrama and Urvashi") by Kalidasa tells the story of mortal King Pururavas and celestial nymph Urvashi who fall in love. As an immortal, she has to return to the heavens, where an unfortunate accident causes her to be sent back to the earth as a mortal with the curse that she will die (and thus return to heaven) the moment her lover lays his eyes on the child which she will bear him. After a series of mishaps, including Urvashi's temporary transformation into a vine, the curse is lifted, and the lovers are allowed to remain together on the earth. Thus these two memorable Sanskrit plays made Kalidasa a worldwide famous playwright and undoubtedly he is often called the Shakespeare of India, though he does not have the range of and variety of Shakespeare, but he has given the world a profounder spiritual vision of life.

Bhavbhuti: Bhavbhuti was an 8th century scholar of India noted for his plays and poetry, written in Sanskrit. His plays are considered equivalent to the works of Kalidasa. Bhavbhuti was born in a Deshastha Brahmin family of Padmapura, Vidarbha, central India, in Gondia district, on Maharashtra and MP border. His real name was Srikantha Nilakantha, and he was the son of Nilakantha and Jatukarni. He received his education at 'Padmapawaya', a place some 42 km South-West of Gwalior. Paramhans Dnyananidhi is known to be his guru. He composed his historical plays at 'Kalpi', a place on banks of river Yamuna.He is believed to have been the court poet of King Yashovarman of Kannauj. Kalhana, the 12th century historian, places him in the entourage of the king, who was defeated by Lalitaditya, King of Kashmir, in 736 AD. 'Mahaviracharita' (The story of highly courageous), depicting the early life of Rama. 'Uttararamacharita' (The story of Rama's later life), depicts Rama's coronation, the abandonment of Sita, and their reunion. The play '**Malatimadhava**' is set in the city of Padmavati. The king desires that his minister's daughter Malati marry a youth called Nandana. Malati is in love with Madhava ever since she saw him and drew his portrait. Madhava reciprocates, and draws a portrait of her in turn. Malati suspects her father's motives in falling in with the King's plans for her. A side plot involves the lovers' friends Makaranda and Madayantika. The latter is attacked by a tiger, and Makaranda rescues her, getting wounded in the process. After numerous travails, all ends well, with the two couples uniting.

Sudraka: Another notable playwright Sudraka, genuinely an Indian king, was wellknown playwright for his monumental drama.

'**Mricchakatika'** (The Little Clay Cart):. He has been identified as Abhira king Indragupta, who used the pen name 'Sudraka'. Among the known dramatic composition of ancient India, the 'Mrichchhakatika' occupies a very high and distinguished position. It is a creation of outstanding brilliance. The Mrichchhatika is a Sanskrit drama written by Sudraka in the 2nd century B.C., in ten Acts based on the story of the love of Charudatta, a prominent but poor inhabitant of Ujjayini, and Vasantasena, an exquisitely beautiful but pure-minded courtesan of the city. The play is full of romance, sex, court intrigue, and comedy. Nevertheless, the plot of the play has numerous twists and turns. The story is about a man named 'Charudatta' and his love for Vasantsena, a rich courtesan or nagarvadhu. The love affair is complicated by a royal courtier who is also attracted towards Vasantsena. The plot is further made complicated by thieves and mistaken identities which ultimately results in a hilarious and entertaining play. This is powerfully documenting the social and political conditions of the time as well as delicately delineating personal emotions. Another major feature is its use of several different Prakrit dialects spoken by the minor characters, the women, and the vidushaka. It also contains much wit, humour, and satire.

The Sanskrit drama is the ultimate foundation of Indian theatre and the success of present Indian theatre is solely dependent on it. The Sanskrit drama flourished in its glory under the patronage of the court and the aristocracy till the 12th century when the Mohammedan intrusion shifted the Sanskrit stage. The glory of Sanskrit drama became a thing of the past in the period of decline when it was divorced gradually from the stage. But still it has relevance in folk theatre at present. The genuine development of Sanskrit drama is ceased down in true sense except its few elements are in still practice. Modern Indian theatre is under the great influence of Western philosophy which neglected the traditional Sanskrit drama tradition. Nevertheless, we cannot deny the importance of Sanskrit drama tradition in the development of Indian theatre.

2

Kalidasa's Abhijnana Sakuntalam: Recognition of Sakuntala

The famous play *Abhijna Sakuntalam*, composed by Kalidasa has been tailored from the original epic which shows in the Adiparva part of *Mahabharata*. It is one of Kalidasa's chief victorious elements as play and has been translated by plentiful scholars. Sakuntala, has been resurrected to a novel existence in this play. The exercise of brilliant story and devotion to theatrical sources of Natyashastra discloses a Sakuntala', who has uniqueness, who seeks a personality and one who develops as a character with love for nature.

Life and Historical Aspect of Kalidasa

1. Kalidasa is observed as one of the utmost poets of Sanskrit Literature who secured enormous fame during his existence. He wrote 3 plays *Mālavikāgnimitram*, *Vikramorvasiya* and *Abhijñānaśakuntalā*in which *Abhijñānaśakuntalā* is his mainly well-known play.
2. Kalidasa composed two epic poems *Kumarasambhavam and Raghuvaṃśa* and minor poems, such as, *Meghadūta* and *Ṛtusaṃhāra*.

Kalidasa's Abhijñānaśakuntalā–Mythical Narrative and Adaptation

1. Kalidasa's *Abhijñānaśakuntalā* is a significant and important play which is considered a masterwork in Sanskrit literature. It has its identity in the world literature and has been translated into several languages is still read wide-reaching after so many century.
2. Kalidasa obtained motivation from an easy story and added sources of Natyashastra in the epic to give a different angle to the epic.

3. Kalidasa did not pursue the layout of introducing the characters in the middle of the Act, only in the starting features are given the inclination of entry and then it is assumed that people will know by the tone of the play, when a nature will penetrate.
4. *Abhijñānaśakuntalā* stands with the tale of two lovers who go through a hard journey to find love. Kalidasa divided the play into seven acts dealing with a prototype of encounter, division and reunion.
5. From Act I to Act III we observe how Dushyanta while hunting in a forest comes across Sage Kanva's hermitage. At the same time as triping the hermitage he observes Sakuntala and is infatuated by her beauty and immediately falls in love but is confused at her being a hermit's daughter.
6. It is noted that Act IV starts with a curse which sage Durvasas gives to Sakuntala for the reviled action that he receives at the Hermitage as a visitor. He gave her a curse that: "Your follower shall forget you though reminded, or think of you as of a tale told".
7. Act IV stands the departure of Sakuntala from her hermitage to find her love and recognition in Hastinapur where her husband King Dushyanta lives.
8. Act V is extremely vital for both the protagonists of the play, as it features their inner features as it sets up the separation between them.
9. Sakuntala disappears with the "heavenly light in women's form, but shining bright." Act VI starts with the understanding the feel affection for that King had for Sakuntala as the fisherman.
10. The final act, Act VII highlights as an amalgamation after the division of both the characters. In this act we observe humankind of religious loveliness".

Kalidasa's Legendary Story and its Variation

1. The very work which has been tailored by Kalidasa from the Indian epic *Mahabharata* by Vyasa has "transformed the somewhat unremarkable original into something multifaceted".
2. Kalidasa's story to makes the protagonist Dushyanta as extremely high-quality nature who is cursed by sage Duravsas is not the story as represented in *Mahabharata*.
3. The feminist viewpoint is widespread in both the narratives and Sakuntala upholds her personality in both the stories.

4. Dushyanta shifts his position and suits a King who is not at error but his fault is governed by paranormal sources.
5. The exceptional *Abhijanasakuntalam* has been so wonderfully prearranged by Kalidasa with the sources of Natyashastra that it is hard to complicate all the complex feelings.
6. There have been unusual understandings other than all consent with the sentiments of Dramaturgy and poetic method engaged by Kalidasa.

Story: Abhijnanasakuntalam

Abhijnanasakuntalam is a beautiful tale of love and romance, the name literally meaning 'Of Sakuntala who is recognized by a token'. Written by one of the greatest poets of India, Sakuntalam is synonymous with its author, Kalidasa. *Abhijnanasakuntalam* is the first Indian play ever to be translated into western languages. It is for the very first time translated in English language by Sir William Jones in the year 1789. Later to this, there were at least 46 translations of this play by Kalidasa in 12 different European languages.

Abhijnanasakuntalam is a play which is divided into seven acts. The title means *"***recognition of Sakuntala***"*. It is the last play by Kalidasa. The play is based on the story of Dushyanta in Adiparav of Mahabharta. The title of the play allows us an entry into the theme of the play which denotes " a play about Shakuntala focusing on her recognition by means of the ring (token.). The play is supposed to be written between 1 B.C. 400 A.D. and is considered as the best work of Kalidasa. *Abhijnanasakuntalam* is inspired from the chapter 62–68 of *Mahabharta*. Kalidasa, keeping in mind the original story, molded the characters in such a way so as to show them as ideal characters. He also introduced different characters like Sakuntala's friends who did serious talking on her part in the play but originally never existed. He also introduces the different dramatic devices such as the ring given to Sakuntala by Dushyant, the curse of Rishi Durvasa to make the characters seem perfect in every role of the play and to shift the blame of their mistakes to the particular device to idealise the characters. In the play, Kalidasa shows the identification of Sakuntala from time and again. In Act 6, a fisherman is arrested by the officers of Dushyanta's kingdom because he was thought of as a thief by the officers. It was so because he had a very precious ring that had king's name engraved on it. The ring is shown to Dushyanta and he immediately recognizes it and feels guilty for the remembering the love of his life, that is Sakuntala and publicly humiliating her. The king is in grief and decides not to celebrate the spring time and kingdom feels gloomy all over. He also paints a painting of Sakuntala which looks exactly like her. In this act, the king is also given a message of the death of a merchant whose wife is pregnant. He orders that all the wealth of the merchant goes to his pregnant wife rather than in the kingdom's treasure, as per rule. He, here also realizes or is again pained with the thought that he has no son and he had lost Sakuntala who was pregnant when he abandoned her.

Abhijnanasakuntalam is a beautiful tale of love and romance. Sakuntala was the daughter of Rishi Vishwamitra and Apsara Menaka. Menaka was sent to distract Vishwamitra during his meditation, by Lord Indra in the fear that Vishwamitra might gain more powers than the Gods if he continues to meditate. Meneka succeeds in distracting him and give birth to their daughter Sakuntala. Vishwamitra abandons both of them, knowing that Menaka cannot take the child up to heaven. He was infuriated by his loss of chastity. Sakuntala was left alone in the forest by Menaka. The birds took care of Baby Sakuntala until sage Kanava took her as his child and named her Sakuntala. These birds were vultures that derives 'Shakun' in Sanskrit and 'tala' means beneath. as the vultures protected her covering with the wings. Sakuntala grows up to be a beautiful young lady just like her mother Meneka. One day, King Dushyant, while on hunt, stops at the hermit's cottage to seek his blessings. He looks at Sakuntala and he is mesmerized by her beauty. But he does not come out of his hiding. He continues to listen to the conversation of Sakuntala with her two friends. He comes out of the hiding only when he is sure of her birth. He comes to know that the sage is not in the cottage at the moment and will come after few days. He accepts the hospitality of Sakuntala and her friends and confesses his love for her and promises her that the son born from her will the heir – apparent of the kingdom. They get into a gandharva marriage and the king is called back to the kingdom because of some work. But he leaves his ring with his name inscribed on it and gives it to Sakuntala as his token of love and also promises to return soon and take Sakuntala with him. Sakuntala is compared to the Green nature again and again in the play. She is as soft, tender and loving as the Mother Nature. She is portrayed as a true beautiful lady.

While the sage Kanva was still not as the cottage was visited by sage Durvasa, who was very well known for his anger. When no one at the cottage attends him he gets angry and curses Sakuntala (seeing as she was the only one in the cottage) that whoever she was thinking about will forget her. But after many pleas by Sakuntala and her friends to the sage, he agrees to omit the curse as he cannot take it back. He says that on offering something to the person she was thinking about that belongs to him (i.e. the ring), he will remember everything. (Sakuntala was thinking about Dushyanata). After months of waiting, when she fails to hear anything from the king, Sage Kanva arranges for the visit of Sakuntala to the royal court of king Dushyanta. On her way she stops to drink water by a lake and unfortunately the ring slips from her finger and swallowed by a fish. She was pregnant with her son here. She reaches the court and Dushyanta praises her beauty but fails to recognize her. She pleads but it is of no use. She ultimately is taken away by same kind of mystical light. Later, the king gets his ring back that he was given to Sakuntala and immediately he feels guilty of not recognizing her and publically humiliating and abandoning her especially when she was pregnant with his own child. He wishes to bring her back and apologize to her and make everything right but he does not know where to start his search from. He becomes a mourning mess. This is where we see the transformation of love to spiritual love from physical love. Dushyanta is also aware of his childless state and all the stress of thinking causes him to fell unconscious. He returns to his consciousness when he hears his friend Madhavya's cries for help. He challenges the enemy to fight him and leave Madhavya but it is not an enemy but Lord Indra's charioteer Matali who has come to take Dushyanta with him to Lord Indra's decree. Dushyanta leaves with Matali to fight the demons in the celestial regions as instructed by Indra, the king of heavens.

After the fulfillment of his mission, Dushyanta ask Matali to stop by hermitage of Marica to get the sage's blessings. There, while waiting for Matali to get the sage's permission to meet him, Dushyanta meets a small boy, playing with the cub. He instantly feels drawn towards him. The two ladies, attending child, on seeing Dushyanta ask him to help them to persuade the child to leave the cub alone but the child does not listen and says that he is not afraid. The child is wearing an amulet and no one other than his parents and sage can touch the child. If done, the amulet would turn into a serpent and bite the person. Dushyanta notices the resemblance between him and the child. He comes to know that the child is of Puru race and his mother's name is Sakuntala. He is then sure of the child as his own and falls to Sakuntala's feet and ask for her forgiveness and also asks her to come back to him with their child. Sakuntala forgives him and they both go to see the sage and seek his blessings. The sage tells him of Rishi Durvasa's curse and thus frees him of his guilt. The sage Marichi and his consort Aditi bless the two with their child Sarvadhaman and give them their love. Thus, the play comes to an end with prayer of Lord Shiva.

Kalidas has an unparalleled reputation as a poet not only in India, but also all over the world. Globalisation opened up its doors to Kalidas' works in 1789 when Sir William Jones translated his play Abhigyan Sakuntalam. These facts will bring you closer to history as well as Kalidas' brilliance.

Theme of Love in Abhigyan Sakuntalam by Kalidasa

'Waiting is a real sign of true love and patience, anyone can say I love you, but not everyone can wait and prove that its true'. These lines are proved true in the play Abhigyana Sakuntalam. It is a beautiful tale of love and romance written by one of the greatest poets of India, Kalidasa, one of the greatest Sanskrit poet that India ever had and his life history is absolutely fascinating and interesting. Perhaps the most famous and beautiful work of his is Sakuntalam. This is a love drama and we can feel love showering throughout the play. Their love brings us on a journey that makes us laugh, cry tears of happiness and sorrow, and even blows us away by their love. This story basically focuses on the theme of love. It centralizes on the thought that 'We are born alone, we live alone, we die alone. Only through our love and friendship can we create the illusion for the moment that we are not alone.' It defines love very well as we can feel a very different kind of sensation in almost every aspect of this play.

According to me love can not only in between a girl and a boy who are planning to get married, infact love is everywhere. It can be between us and god or between us and our parents. Similarly even in this play when sage kanava spotted the new born child, surrounded by Sakuntala birds then taken by kindness, he decides to take the child home and name her Sakuntala. This shows how love does not bothers about blood relation or anything and can make someone adopt a child out of love.

Even when we move further in this play, we can see how Sakuntala grows up to be a beautiful woman just like her mother Menaka. One day, King Dushyant, while returning from a deer hunt, happens to stop by the hermit's cottage. There he saw Sakuntala engaged in a friendly banter with her friends. Sakuntala found her deer whimpering in pain and tried to comfort it. Sakuntala very much loved the animals of the forest and her attachment for the animal touched Dushyanta's heart and he asked her to forgive him for his cruel behaviour. She forgives him and he asks to stay in the forest for a few days to tend the wounded deer. They fell in love and they decided to marry.

Their love was so deep that the inner joy of Dushyanta and of the beauty of Sakuntala triggers the feeling of love in him. Though standing behind the bushes he too is unable to control himself from adoring and appreciating Sakuntala's magical youth. On the proposal of marriage Sakuntala asked the king to wait for the sage kanava to return, but the strong love between them did not let them wait as both of them were willing to marry this is when in the absence of the sage, they secretly married in the ceremony of "Gandharva Vivaha" with Mother Nature as the witness.

After some days, the King got news of unrest in his city and is summoned to return. He leaves sadly, but promises to return soon and take his beloved with him. As a token of love, he gives her a signet ring and promises to send an envoy to escort her to the palace. But then the king did not kept his promise and from here begins the waiting period of Sakuntala which is the actual test of her true love. Sakuntala waits for dushyanta's people to come and take her to his palace. But they never do.

Every love story is not always a straight road which means that in every love story the lovers have to face many difficulties to get their love and become one. It is not always easy to achieve what you want and one needs to fight for his or her love. Same was in the case of Sakuntala. She was already suffering from so much pain of separation and waiting, but as said earlier it is not easy to get one's love, so here comes one more obstacle.

One day, sage Durvasa, famous for anger, stops by the hut for hospitality. Lost in her love thoughts, Sakuntala fails to acknowledge his presence. This rises the temperamental sage and he curses Sakuntala, that the one whom she is thinking about will forget her. Sakuntala begs for mercy and explains her situation. On the plea of Sakuntala and her friends, the sage agrees and says that if the king sees any significant thing that he gave her, he will remember everything.

Now we again are confronted with the love of sage Kanava towards Sakuntala. When he returned he knew by his spiritual insight that Sakuntala and Dushyanta were united by gandharva vivaaha and his daughter was pregnant. The sage puts his seal approval on the marriage as divinely ordained and, in due course Sakuntala delivers a male child. After so many months of waiting, when she fails to hear anything from the king, Sage Kanava arranges for the visit of Sakuntala to the court of King Dushyant. On her way, she stops by a lake to drink water and unfortunately the ring slips out of her finger and suddenly a fish swallows it. She reaches the royal palace, but Dushyant did not recognized her because of the curse given to her earlier. She then remembers the ring but realizes that she has lost it somewhere. With disappointment, she returns back to the forest.

As it is very well said that never lose hope and if there is true love then one can even change the lines of destiny from his or her hand. This belief was proved true because at the time when Sakuntala was very disappointed then all of a sudden a miracle happened and the angler came in the play as if he is a messenger of the God. In the play after sometime, an angler finds the ring in the stomach of a fish. He immediately takes it to the king, who on seeing the ring recalls everything and rushes to the hermitage to meet Sakuntala. There they reunite. At that time this is the message of kanava to Dushyanta concerning Sakuntala: "considering us hermits whose only wealth is tapasya, your own birth in a noble family, the love of Sakuntala for you in bringing about which her relatives had no role, you, as her husband, should give her an equal status and love among your wives. Anything beyond this will depend on her bhaagya or luck, the relatives of the bride have no say about that."

At the end of the play, one feels sad at the sufferings of Sakuntala and we are at a loss as to whether we should blame Dushyanta or the divine power for these happenings. Though young in age, she speaks but a few words in profound sense. One wonder at the manner in which she has transformed herself from a pleasure seeking woman imbued with a sense of total renunciation and service. Through portraying scenes of Sakuntala's maids teasing her, sage Kanava's far sightedness, the king's paining for Sakuntala's love when she is away, Sakuntala's unlimited sense of love, the devine grace which brought about the happy reunion, all these presents us an image of victory of true love. Everything happens for a reason. Even in this play, from starting to end it was the power of love which was influencing in all the situations. Whether it was the situation of a new born child surrounded by Sakuntala birds or the fish which had swallowed the signet ring, all these played a very important role in the contribution of love.

All this was possible only because of the love, patience and trust of Sakuntala. If she would have given up then it was almost impossible for them to reunite. It was the true love of Sakuntala because of which even the nature and others around her helped her to succeed. This proves that true love never dies. If one has strong determination to achieve something then he or she will surely succeed. It teaches us a fact that one needs to have faith on your love, and should not leave the sensitive rope of hope. One single mistake may loosen the grip of love and trust from your relationship. It is very well said that if you desire something from the heart then the whole universe will work towards getting you that.

3
Mahabharata: Selections from the Epic

The *Mahabharata* is usually accepted as an encyclopedia of ancient Indian culture and civilization, next in importance only to the Vedas, and is often referred to as the fifth Veda.

Although the central narrative of the epic is the struggle for power between the Kauravas and the Pandavas, the content of the poem is vast and varied. Its structure is very intricate. It's content has passages of philosophical poetry, poetry of the metaphysical imagination, and its appeal ranges from the purely literal to the highly symbolic and spiritual. There is the physical Kurukshetra and there is the Kurukshetra of the mind. In certain passages of great depth, it speaks of the subtle form of the soul and sets forth in detail, the many paths that are open for soul experience.

Vyasa who is considered the composer of The *Mahabharata* unravels the mystery of the animal creation, of the Veda which is wisdom itself, of Yoga with all its metaphysical background of wealth, Desire and Duty. He includes the wisdom of various disciplines or sciences like Ayurveda, Dhanurveda or the science of the bow, Sthapatyaveda or the science of architecture and engineering, and many others.

That the *Mahabharata* was intended as a grand treatise on life is indicated when Vyasa tells

Brahma in The *Mahabharata* itself:

> I have in this epic clarified the mystery of the Vedas and incorporated the very essence of all the Shastras or sacred lores as well as the essence of the six constituents of the Vedas and of the Upanishads. I have packed full into it history and legendary lore. There is matter in it regarding the three dimensions of time - past, present and future. I have spoken authoritatively in the epic about the form and features of old age, death, fear and disease, and about the truth and illusoriness of things. I have clearly explained in it various religious requirements, the distinguishing features of the four ashramas or stages of life, the duties incumbent upon the

> members of the four castes, and the basic philosophy of the Puranas. In this monumental work, I have also discoursed on the nature of Penance and Abstinence, the manner in which they are to be observed, and the fruits thereof. Embedded also in it are accounts of the earth, sun, moon, stars and mini-stars, the duration and scale of the four yugas or Ages (Krta, Treta, Duapara and Kali) and the spiritual contents figuring in the four Vedas. Presented in detail in it are the science of the proper articulation and pronunciation of Vedic texts, therapeutics or the science of medicine, charity and the doctrine related to Siva. The reasons why souls take body in the wombs of gods, men, animals and birds are also set forth in this work. There is description in it of holy places, regions, rivers, mountains, forests, seas, glorious cities, the construction of forts, the skill in arms of ancient kings and of various languages and castes rarely known. There are aphorisms and proverbs here which are useful to people in their daily life. Nor has this work left out an account of the absolute dwelling in the heartcaves of all living beings. (*The Mahabharata*)

Brahma replies to Vyasa and pays his own tribute to the encyclopedic epic, saying.

> "You have been a spokesman of God and dedicated the epic to the enthronement of Truth. You have called the Monumental work composed by you an epic and it is as an epic, therefore, that it will be known. No great world poet, whatever his greatness, will be able to compose an epic greater than yours." (*The Mahabharata*)

2. Evolution of the *Mahabharata*

You are aware that The *Mahabharata* is an epic—a 'Mahakavya'. But as students of literature, we must remember that this epic began as an itihasa, a primarily historical work. Only, the method of its transmission was oral. It was passed on from generation to generation. Bards, minstrels, rhapsodists are all people associated with the tradition of oral transmission in times when the written form was rare and difficult to prepare or procure. An eminent scholar Dandekar, talking about *The Mahabharata* says:

It appears to me that the historical basis of the *Mahabharata* is quite slender, diffuse and not easily identifiable. A commonplace family feud is subjected to epic magnificationwith all its hyperboles, miracles, mystification, symbolization, idealization and universalisation. The *Mahabharata*, I submit, is essentially an epic poem- with emphasis on both the words 'epic' and 'poem'- and not a historical document in the restricted sense of the term. So, in a sense, it is an epic born out of an 'itihasa'.

Now, when we look at it as an epic poem we need to understand its evolution. In order to come to terms with the vastness of the epic we would do well to remember that the *Mahabharata* is over eight times the combined length of the western epics of classical literature, the Iliad and the Odyssey. It is, in its present form perceived as a blend of history and mythology and constitutes an outstanding record of the collective conscious, unconscious and sub-conscious of man However, it is generally accepted among scholars that it evolved over three stages of composition and compilation. An eminent scholar, Professor U.K. Gokak tells us that "Jaya" was the name given to Vyasa's itihasa. The text composed by Vyasa was named Jaya referring to the triumph of good, the victory of the Pandavas. This original composition had about eight thousand stanzas and was recited by Vyasa to his son Suka.

3. Narrative Technique

The evolution of the *Mahabharata* described in the preceding segment has a direct bearing on the narrative technique of this epic. Considering the immensity of its inclusive range, the *Mahabharata* is considered a Book of Books. The vastness of its time frame which includes several generations justifies the many narrators of the poem. You may note that in a sense, it begins with the end. Descendants of the Pandavas, having been persuaded not to perform the Yogya for mass killing of serpents wish to hear about the glory of their ancestors. The *Mahabharata* is a highly enhanced narrative of the glory of the entire clan, the descendants of **Shantanu** and **Satyavati**. The two rival factions, the **Pandavas** and the **Kauravas**, stand for two polarized aspects of the moral perception of life, material and spiritual. In the process of expressing this expansive world view, the epic has to resort to multiple narrators and narrative methods.

The most obvious aspect to be noted is that the final narrator **Ugrasravas** refers every now and then to the person whose recitation he depends upon. Vaishampayana said" is his way of telling the listeners that his narrative is an old narrative of history, folklore, mythology that has come down to him through generations. Having listeners ask questions is a method of giving the narrator/ rhapsodist a chance to bring in more content, philosophical, spiritual or material. More stories, more characters, a greater range of material is thus included in the recitation. This is often described by critics as the practice of having stories within stories and yet more stories. There are plots and sub-plots and sub-sub-plots.

At this point it is pertinent to recall the names of the known narrators of the epic narrative.

— There is **Vyasa** the original composer and narrator for whom Ganesha was the scribe.
— The next significant narrator was **Vaishampayana** who narrated Vyasa's tale to Janmejaya, the great-grandson of the Pandava, Arjuna.
— This narrative was overheard by a Santi or bard called Romaharshana who passed it on to his son **Ugrasravas** who narrated it to Shaunaka and other sages of the Naimisha forest.

Coming to the narrators within the narrative itself, we have the very interesting role of Sanjaya who is endowed with the divine gift of divya drishti which enables him to describe, in great detail, the action taking place on the battle field of Kurukshetra. He describes the war to the blind Dhritarashtra and indirectly to us too as modern day readers/listeners. Within the framework of lineage and caste, Sanjaya himself was a bard. The minstrels who narrated the epic were known as 'sutas'.

'Sutas' were the illegitimate offspring of Kshatriya royalty. For instance, Karna and Vidura are intelligent people, sons of royalty, but are called Sutas. 'Karna is a major character in the epic. He is the son of Kunti and the Sun god but, abandoned by Kunti, is raised by a charioteer. Vidura, the most dispassionate royal advisor to the Kauravas, half-brother of Dhritarashtra, is the son of a royal maid and Vyasa. Both these characters are examples of 'Sutas'.

4. Stories Adding Meaning to a Narrative

A popular yet serious narrative like the *Mahabharata* necessarily contains abstract ideas.

Stories enable a narrator to convey those abstract ideas in situational terms so that in the event of an oral recitation they are understood immediately and instantly. Critics who try to explain the power of stories say that like fiction or poetry, stories enable us to experience feelings, thoughts, emotions and images which may lie dormant in our subconscious mind.

In a sense, stories reflect a part of our inner selves, helping us to understand and heal ourselves. Complex and difficult experiences of life can be conveyed through stories.

5. The Organic Unity of the *Mahabharata*

There has been endless comment on the diversity of the *Mahabharata*. There are no limitations of time, place or action but it has also been conceived as a tree which grows out of a seed and grows with its roots spreading underground and its branches spreading in every direction. In his commentary on the *Mahabharata*, Vidya Niwas Misra gives a detailed analogy:

> The conceptualization as a tree signifies one thing, namely, that all material within the epic is organically related and is one totality. Nothing is grafted from outside. The main trunk of the story lends itself to branch out into sub-stories. The seed of poetic structure remains one. The trunk is one, the major branches are defined and well developed, only they continue to leaf out and blossom. When the fruit forms, the tree achieves its final shape- the tree of the *Mahabharata*. Whatever additions or deletions take place, they happen before fruition.

6. The Moral Framework of the *Mahabharata*

i. Dharma

David Crystal in the Cambridge Paperback Encyclopedia describes dharma as, "In Hinduism, the universal law that applies to the Universe, human society, and the individual. It is both a general code of ethics applicable to all, and a moral law specific to an individual's station in life."

Yudhishtira, the protagonist of the *Mahabharata* is the son of Dharma and himself Dharma incarnate. He is constantly faced with dilemmas but always applies the test of dharma to his actions. Critics have pointed out that this epic is not essentially about courage, valour or physicalnprowess but about spiritual strength, flexibility and the ability to face life courageously.

Yudhishtira's judgment and commitment to Dharma are tested time and again but he always abides by Dharma. The Yaksha of the lake puts him through a trial but in both thought and action, he is able to satisfy the embodiment of Dharma: his answers to the Yaksha are steeped in acceptance of the universal law and his choice of his youngest step Madri's brother, Sahdev, Madri's son as the one to be brought back to life, reveal his commitment to the principles of Dharma.

So does his willingness to bear the consequences of his choice, even if it is an unfairly inflicted and unfairly won game of dice. The episode of Yudhishtira standing at the gates of heaven in his earthly body with a dog in tow is known to all. His refusal to enter without the dog is an act of dharma. He refuses to abandon his companion, thus abiding by Dharma.

Coming back to the "universal law" of Crystal's definition, the *Mahabharata* shows us that the truth of an individual, of a society, of a community or of a nation has to be in consonance with cosmic and universal truth. It cannot be merely theorized. Dharma is put to test in everyday life, and there is no absolute dharma. The dharma of crisis situations is different from the dharma of everyday life. If an action contributes to universal good, it conforms to dharma even if it does not conform to societal norms. When choices are to be made between conflicting dharmas, a great deal of thought, concentration and judgment have to be exercised.

ii. Destiny

The *Mahabharata* depicts the suffering of the righteous man. On the face of it the epic appears to believe that the irreversible destiny of man is to suffer. But, very perceptively the scholar Vidya Niwas Misra points out there is a notion of the destined, but only to dramatize human weakness. One who is not willing to face suffering as a consequence of his own action makes a scapegoat of destiny. When suffering is unbearable, blaming fate is a big help. When Draupadi comes to Kunti for blessings, Kunti says: "Daughter, give birth to sons with good fate and stars. Do not give birth to the ones who are merely brave and learned. My sons are both brave and learned, but not fortunate. They are wandering in the jungles helplessly." This admonition does not mean that Kunti wants cowards and dullards as her grandsons. It only points to her unbearable anguish at the fate her sons have met. Won't they ever know peace and happiness, she wonders! This instance is not a validation of destiny. It is only an expression of anguish.

If destiny does take its course in the *Mahabharata*, it is due to some karmic deed of one's own. If a curse is inflicted, that curse is self earned by some slip or folly. Acting judiciously brings peace of mind and makes suffering bearable. A conscientious person introspects to see if he has made compromises or whether he has bowed to someone who is unjust, for personal promotion. He experiences contentment even if he gets a little without causing suffering to others, without aligning with villains or giving up the path of virtue.

In the *Mahabharata*, 'Yudhishtira's willingness to accept just five villages for himself and his Pandava brothers is a case in point. But his efforts to avoid a full-fledged conflict with the

Kauravas prove futile as Duryodhana is unwilling to give them even a needle point of land.

The *Mahabharata* teaches us that the vices of envy, lust, anger, greed, pride and attachment are quick to propagate but produce impermanent results. Godly virtues, though slow to grow, are lasting. In the ultimate analysis, the path to Moksha lies through fortitude and forbearance.

7. The Dicing: A Detailed Study

(i) This is one of the sections of the epic listed for detailed study. As such you should be able to explain any lines or episodes even if you see them in isolation. For this, we need to keep some things in mind. Recall what was mentioned in the Introduction. Remember that what we are reading is Ugrasravas's rendering of the *Mahabharata*. That is why you often see, "Vaishampayana again said—"Ugrasravas is quoting Vaishampayana who is repeating what Yudhishtira or Draupadi or Duryodhana or Dhritarashtra or Vidur or any of the other characters said in the assembly.

Coming to the book itself, let us place it in sequential perspective. Having set up a capital in a new city at Khandavprastha which they render into Indraprastha as opposed to Hastinapur over which the Kauravas preside, Yudhishtira establishes suzerainty over a very large number of barons (rulers) in north India. He then seeks to legitimize his authenticity by performing a Rajsuya Yagya to which all the barons of various Kingdoms are invited and pay tribute in acknowledgement of Yudhistiras supremacy. The only two states/rulers from whom tribute is not received are king Dhrupada (father of Draupadi, and an ally, by marriage, of the Pandavas) and Krishna who had helped the Pandavas to slay Sisupala, the powerful king who had subdued 86 out 101 barons of aryan lineage in Northern India of those times, i.e. in the second millenium B.C. When the Pandavas hold such an important ceremony as a Rajsuya Yagya it is natural that their Kaurava cousins from Hastinapur are also invited. However the visit leaves the Kauravas jealous at the sheer wealth amassed and the splendour of the new capital, its palace and hall. After all, Dhritrashtra had sent them away to seek a new life from scratch in Khandavaprastha. They had done well and with the help of Maya, a demon who was also an architect, set up a splendid capital. It is after this visit that Duryodhana descends into a sulk and when asked, reveals to Sakuni, his maternal uncle, the cause of his unhappiness. As it is revealed that jealousy over the wealth and property of his Pandava cousins is the cause of Duryodhana's unhappiness, the cunning, scheming Sakuni devises the ploy of inviting them to a game of dice to defraud them of their wealth. The plan is conveyed to Dhritrashtra who has to give permission for the game of dice to be held in the assembly hall in the presence of the family elders and other important people. He is initially hesitant but is subsequently prevailed upon to dispatch Vidura with the invitation. Many questions have been asked about why Yudhistira accepted, bu the answer seems to be that he was simply following a code of conduct or a social convention which dictated that a game of dice could not be declined. Van Buitenen in his introduction to the *Mahabharata* indicates that dicing is a part of the rajasuya rituals when he says "Yudhishtira had not so far been at all fond of gambling— we have seen quite a bit of him now—and can hardly be regarded as under a private compulsion to rise to any game". Nevertheless, he submits, though grudgingly: "Once challenged, I cannot refuse." Once we accept the dicing as an integral part of rajasuya, in the Assembly Hall, as well as the ritual manuals, Yudhishtira is not at all the statue with the clay feet, the paragon of rectitude with the sudden tragic flaw. The text itself does not condemn Yudhishtira for his gaming. Of course if the gambling had been outside Yudhishtira's universe of law, the authors could easily have dropped the game from their version of the rajasuya, but in a way this would have gone against the spirit of the *Mahabharata* as a whole. It has often been remarked that the epic is a series of precisely stated problems imprecisely and therefore inconclusively resolved, with every resolution raising a new problem, until the very end, when the question remains: whose is heaven, and whose is hell? The point counterpoint is typical of the assembly hall as well: suzerainty achieved, and then gambled away. Rather than dropping the Dicing or treating it as perfunctorily as do the ritual manuals, the authors have seized upon the dicing rite of the vedic ceremony as a ritually legitimate, even prescribed, way of swinging the doubt from Yudhishtiras apparently unassailable position to the claims of the Kauravas. With a masterly stroke of composition the dead letter of the Vedic game is dramatically revived. Mean-while Yudhishtra remains the king Dharma he had not been too happy before about. For this ambition to become samrat, he is now prepared to go the bitter end.

And bitter it is. After an epical losing streak he finds himself obliged to stake his brothers, himself, and Draupadi—obliged, it seems, by the rules of the game, which unfortunately are never explained. What we do gather, however, is those two parties, rather than two individuals play, for Duryodhana's uncle Sakuni may play for him; it is Duryodhana who pays in the stake.

The two parties pay in the first stake in the same amount. The loser adds to his state while the winner's presumably remains the same. It is not clear whether the entire stake stays in the game or the winner pockets the loser's last stake after each play.

Never stated but implicit is this game's rule that it will go through twenty plays which are presented as two phases of ten each. In the first ten plays Yudhishtira forfeits most of his possessions, and after the tenth Vidura, the benevolent uncle of the Pandavas makes an impassioned plea that the game be stopped. Vidura urges not Yudhishtira but Duryodhana's father to stop it and vilifies Duryodhana for persisting in it. This would make no sense if Vidura considered Yudhishtira a free agent; it makes excellent sense if Yudhishtira is bound by the rules of his own Rajasuya and must rise to the challenge.

The game is carried on for another session of ten plays. Yudhishtra first loses untold millions in the eleventh play, in the twelfth all his cattle, in the thirteenth all his land, in the fourteenth the sons of Draupadi by the five Pandavas, in the fifteenth Nakula, in the sixteenth Sahadeva, in the seventeenth Bhima, in the eighteenth Arjuna, in the nineteenth himself. At the twentieth play the final one of the game, Yudhishtira stakes Draupadi. The audience groans and protests but does nothing to stop the play; evidently the game is to be a complete one, with a total winner and a total loser. But our authors, masters of doubt, have already planted a doubt.

Draupadi is lost; she is subjected to indignities that shout for vengeance, she is disrobed but the power of her virtue replaces her sari; she also poses the ultimate riddle. Had Yudhishtira staked and lost himself, she asks, before he staked me? If so, he had lost his freedom and, as a slave of the Kauravas, no longer owned her to stake. After much inconclusive argument, Dhritrashtra rules that the last play was indecisive and that the game as a whole had been neither lost nor won. So the Pandavas depart, free and still rich men. It is clear that the undecided game is not over, only interrupted. At this point if becomes predictable that when the game goes on, it will be with a repeat of the twentieth play which had been inconclusive and that there will be a single deciding play for an all-or-nothing stake between the two branches of the family.

So, promptly there follows the anudyuta, the follow up game, in which Duryodhana, with his father's consent decides to stake Hastinapur against Indraprastha. It is the final moment of truth: this time not the slow attrition of possessions but an instant play of identity. Yudhishtira cannot refuse, for he is under the ritual obligation. But the authors keep the story going. The play is not quite an all or nothing play, but close enough. The stake is victory against twelve year exile in the forest followed by one year of living in the open without being discovered. Yudhistira loses and the next thirteen years are another story.

Having tried to understand the socio-cultural context of dicing, we are still left puzzled by Draupadi's plight in this episode. To understand how she is affected by Yudhishtira's losing her, we need to take a look at the status of women in Aryan society of these times. The aryans who settled in North India after arriving there from Central Asia took the darker skinned natives captive and made them their slaves. In the Atharvaveda, dasi is the term used to describe alien domestic help. There is reference to the black dasi too. The term dasa or dasi thus originally had ethnic connotations although enslaved women in addition to domestic help could also be asked to provide sexual services.

In the *Mahabharata*, the ethnic dimension is not in evidence. A dasa/dasi denotes a human being under the complete control of a master. How did people become dasas or dasis? The *Mahabharata* tells us about enslavement as a result of bet or as a result of defeat in gambling as in the case of Draupadi in the Sabha Parva. Women who were born in the family of slaves were also treated as such. Draupadi laments in the Sabha Parvan that with the enslavement of the Pandavas their children too would be considered slaves. Dasa-bharya is the term used (Dhritarashtra uses this term for Draupadi) for the wife of the slave. This phrase probably implied the reduction into slavery of a free woman if she got married to a slave or was, by circumstances (like Yudhistira) reduced to slavery. A dasi was in no way protected from the unreasonable demands of her master. Dushsasana tells Draupadi in the Sabha Parvan. "Your husbands have lost you, henceforth you are only a dasi and you will have to serve the Kaurvas now. He further says, "It does not matter whether you are badly dressed or not dressed at all, you will have to come with me." Duryodhana could openly invite Draupadi to come and sit on his lap. Draupadi's question regarding whether Yudhisthira had staked and lost himself before he staked her, has a background to it. A dasa/dasi had no right to personal belongings. So even in a culture where wives were 'owned' by their husbands, Draupadi could spot a "loophole" to avoid the disgrace in store for her. A dasi had to perform all types of tasks for her master and his household. Duryodhana demands that Draupadi take off her rich attire and assume that of a menial and clean his palace.

What sets the dasi apart from male slaves is that the dasi could also be asked to provide sexual services. That this fear of sexual violation of a dasi was very real is evident from Yudhistira's concern about how Draupadi would fare in Virata's palace where she would be under the guise of Sairandhri.

Another significant problem that the wise Draupadi touches upon is regarding her son Prativindhya. When she is offered a boon by Dhritarashtra she asks for the freedom of her husbands. One of the reasons she mentions is that she does not want her son to be known as the son of a slave. He has been the son of a king and it seems unbearable that he might be reduced to being the son of a slave. The first boon procures the freedom of Yudhisthira, the second that of Bhimasena, Arjuna, Nakul and Sahdev. She declines a third boon. Even in that patriarchal society, a woman becomes the last refuge of her five husbands.

(ii) The Sequel to the Dicing

This section, as you can see, is much shorter than 'The Dicing'. Whereas the earlier section is a vital one in the plot of the story this one gives us a number of clues to the direction the story will take. Also, it is a peculiar combination of psychological traits, human behaviour and weaknesses and a great deal of philosophising about life and human wrong doing. There are passages which contain expositions of Hindu ritual and the vows and prophecies of the Pandavas and Draupadi give us clues about the future. Vidura, endowed with divyadrishti foretells a gloomy future and Dhirtrashtra is torn between paternal love and fair play. Gandhari like other women in the epic (Kunti, Draupadi) is the one sane voice who knows her son Duryodhana very well and is apprehensive because of the terrible portents that had accompanied his birth. His frequent references to destiny add to the fatalistic perspective which surfaces from time to time in the epic. Even the mighty Drona with whom the entire Kaurava clan seek refuge, seems like a victim of his own destiny condemned to die at the hands of Drupada, a king whom he had deprived of his kingship.

8. The Game of Dice in Relation to the Plot

The question that often comes to mind is, "Why does the game of dice have such a crucial significance in the *Mahabharata* ?" After all anywhere, anyone who knows the least bit about The *Mahabharata* knows about the game of dice, about Yudhishthira, Duryodhana, Shakuni and the loss of the Kingdom, the brothers, and the beloved wife Draupadi. Everyone also knows that

Shakuni was a trickster, Duryodhana greedy cruel prince, Dhritarashtra, a partisan guardian, Bhishma an impotent head of disintegrating clan.

Let us look at the various reasons which render this episode to crucial. The first thing to note is the absence of Krishna during the game of dice. Krishna has been a visible and significant presence during the Rajasuya yagya and has been the guest of honour. He has been present in the earlier part of the book of the assembly hall but is absent during the climax, the game of dice. His absence is explained by his required presence to settle important war business with Sambha who had assaulted Dvaraka. This whole sequence of Krishna's presence and absence can be seen as the work of poet contributors who wished to glorify and deify him. After all the historical Krishna was just a chieftain, brother of Balram, and lord of Dwarka. The religious deity can be seen here in the process of evolution. When Krishna is absent things go horribly wrong and even the desperate calling out to him prevents, somewhat, Draupadi's shame." The Rajasuya of

Yudhisthira has been made an occasion to glorify Krishna. He is not quite the God yet — at least not by Bhagavadgita standards—but his incipient godhead already requires his absence from situations that he cannot dominate." (van Buitenen). Had he attended the dicing no doubt he would have interfered on behalf of the Pandavas, which would have meant the end of the game, and thus, in effect, the end of the *Mahabharata*.

To examine this question, we have to remind ourselves that the epic is an itihas purana— a work of art—a poetic composition. However, the poetic skills of the composer/composers are so highly developed that we have before us a very dramatic climax. It is like the climatic scene or episode of a play. The plot hinges upon this scene. The tragic action is precipitated henceforth. All the major characters are exposed for what they are. Their dialogues are revelatory. Whatever hypocrisy might have lain dormant in the self-righteous Bhishma or Dhritarashtra is revealed, as is their impotence in the face of a rash and impatient Duryodhana. So while on the one hand this scene exposes the male characters, on the other hand it makes us acutely aware of the limitations of women, even royal women like Draupadi.

It is also a scene which brings together Draupadi & Krishna conveying a double lesson, as subsequent myths of sati Draupadi indicate. Draupadi is depicted and worshipped in later cults as the model of the intelligent and loyal wife. Her chastity (satitva) has the power to prevent her shame. On the other hand it enables the performance of a miracle by Krishna, the endless lengthening of her sari as Duryodhana tries to strip her in the Sabha. This episode actually provides drama, thrill, villainy, excitement, which are very obvious to us because of the advantage of media exposure which we have unlike earlier readers of the epic.

So far, we have seen the tangible ways in which the Dicing is crucial to the rest of the *Mahabharata*. There is yet another vital point to note on the matter. That relates to the philosophy and the religious dimension of the epic.

If there had been no game of Dice, there would have been no humiliation of the Pandavas and molestation of Draupadi. Had these not taken place, the provocation for all the vows of bringing destruction upon the Kauravas and their allies would have been lost. Draupadi's violent curses and Bhima's vows of revenge are rooted in this episode. Within the larger context of the epic there is a large number of characters who have to fulfil their destiny and it is the *Mahabharata* war, which will provide the opportunity. The Shikandi—Bhishma struggle, Drona's death and various other scores are settled in the war resulting from the Kauravas' refusal to hand over legitimate power and property to the Pandavas.

It is in the war whose seeds were sown at the game of Dice that the most profound religious discourse of all time was recited. The Bhagavadgita, the ultimate treatise on man's conduct in life, was actually a counselling lecture to Arjun by Lord Krishna when Arjun is reduced to inaction at the prospect of fighting his own brethren. I am sure you do not miss the religious stature of the Krishna who began as a political manipulator and chieftain in the early books of the epic.

From the point of view of the whole epic, the episode picks up threads from the books of the earlier part, but more significantly it prepares the reader for the action of the subsequent books. It provides a catalyst for the resolution to all the conflicts referred to in the earlier parts of the epic. In the process it reverberates in a transgenerational framework. This means that the action affects and is brought about, by more than two generations. The most obvious character whose life spans a long period of time is Bhishma who has seen Satyawati, Vichitravirya, Dhritarashtra, Duryodhana and his descendants. In fact the events of the game of dice cast their shadow on the characters right up to the gates of heaven i.e., their death.

9. Sabha Parva or the Book of the Assembly Hall

The Book of the Assembly Hall is the pivotal one of the eighteen Major Books of the *Mahabharata*: it is also one of the more diversified and interesting ones [J.A.B. van Buitenen, "On the Structure of the Sabhaparvan of the *Mahabharata*", in India Maior (Festschrift Gonda), Leyden, 1972, pp.68-84]. In the Critical Edition, this second of the eighteen Maha Parvas has a total of 9 Upa Parvas (Sections), 72 Chapters and 2390 Shlokas.

For all its length and variety, Adi Parva – the Book of the Beginning- has not done more than lay the groundwork of the epic. It was more or less a closed whole: the ancestry of the protagonists and antagonists; their youth, early strife, and clouded claims on the succession; the attempts at assassination, and the safe deliverance of the Pandavas; their self-exile and glorious reappearance at Draupadi's bridegroom choice; their consequent marriage, alliance with Panchala, and recognition by the senior Kauravas; and finally the acquisition of the kingdom of Indraprastha by the partition of the Field of the Kurus. Peace was restored in the end between the two branches of siblings through the wise guidance of their elders. One might well close The Beginning and never expect a sequel to it.

But the Assembly Hall makes all that went before just a beginning. Those were the pages of childhood and adolescence, in which the influence of the elders was strong and decisive. Now the heroes are on their own and begin to act in their own right; and their natures are willful. The Sabha Parva begins with establishing Yudhishthira and his brothers as prosperous princeling at Indraprastha. But this is not much: so far the Pandavas have simply acquired a new home base. Now, at the suggestion of a visiting messenger of the Gods – though not sent by the Gods – the seer Narada, Yudhishthira conceives the desire to perform the ancient Vedic ritual of the Rajasuya – the Royal Consecration. This, at first glance, appears as no more than the legitimization of his new, and so to say supernumerary, kingship by means of the old rite. It transpires, however, that there is much more to it than that; for through it Yudhishthira wishes to aspire to nothing less than universal sovereignty by becoming Samraj, an "all-king" or "emperor", to whom all other princes of the land will be submissive.

It is not at all clear on what personal accomplishments Yudhishthira could pretend to rest such a claim. After all, he has allowed himself to be ousted from the ancestral seat of Hastinapura in return fro a parcel of wilderness that still had to be cleared. True, he has won the alliance of Panchala, but merely by marriage. The end of Adi Parva has left us with the mild satisfaction that some attractive noble youths, after some bad luck and some good, in the end did not fare so ill. But imperial ambitions all of a sudden? Still, perhaps his ambition stood in need of no justification; for he is to embark on a grand Vedic ceremony, the Rajasuya, and to qualify for it the performer's intention may suffice.

Once his desire has taken hold, Yudhisthira calls in Krishna of the Vrishnis for counsel. He had already pointed out the obvious: the performance requires the "unanimity of the baronage" to be tributary to him. For the Rajasuya, as it is presented in this Parva is not just the installation of anew king, it is the glorification of a king of kings. There can only be one such suzerain at the time. So it requires not only the assent of the baronage, but also the removal of the present suzerain. The one *en titre* is Jarasandha, the king of the more eastern land of Magadha, a populous and prosperous realm. So Jarasandha is indeed removed, and the rest of the world, not excluding Rome and Antioch and the "city of the Greeks", is made tributary. After the assassination of Jarasandha the performance takes place, but is it not concluded without resistance. While Yudhishthira's preeminence is never disputed, the high ranking of Krishna is. The challenger, Shishupala, is eliminated by Krishna, and Yudhisthira is suzerain indeed: but for a brief while. The title is wrested from him by the Hastinapura Kauravas in a game of dice, when Yudhishthira loses on pain of an exile of thirteen years.

Most of the proceedings of this Parva take place in an assembly hall, a kind of longhouse for the men in which to hold council and entertainment, and it is from such a hall that the Parva takes its title. There are two halls involved, the one at Indraprastha and that at Hastinapura. It is Indraprastha hall that becomes a bone of contention; it is in the Hastinapura hall where it all ends.

The hall at Indraprastha was newly built by an Asura, Maya by name, who had been saved from the fire of the Khandava Forest, which concluded the Adi Parva. So magnificent was that hall that it excited the envy of Kaurava's cousin Duryodhana, and this envy led to the game at dice on whose outcome the rest of the *Mahabharata* hangs. When Yudhishthira has reached the pinnacle of temporal power as the acknowledged suzerain of all the world, he is challenged to the game. Why he felt he had to accept the challenge is a question that is not fully addressed in the Parva. It is sufficed to note, however, that there is a conspicuous thread in the Parva: the settlement in Indraprastha needs a hall – the hall needs validation as a royal court through the Royal Consecration – it evokes the others' envy – and brings about a game in another hall where Yudhishthira loses all.

Clearly therefore the structure of Sabha Parva is much tighter than that of the Adi Parva, where the insertions and additions are quite obvious. The Sabha Parva too has its fuzzy edges: Narada's long instruction in policy and administration is a clear instance. But otherwise the Parva hangs together remarkably well.

It has been said that this Parva is pivotal to the *Mahabharata* as a whole. The remaining epic can almost be predicted in outline: there are to follow thirteen years of exile and the adventures thereof, described in the Vana Parva, the Book of the Forest and Virata Parva, the Book of Virata. It is likely that the molestation of the Pandavas' wife Draupadi at the hands of Duhshasana and Duryodhana will remain unavenged? Or that Duryodhana will surrender half the kingdom to Yudhishthira when he returns? We see looming The Book of the Effort (Udyoga Parva), and the war books of Bhishma, Drona, Karna, Shalya and the rest.

10. Temptation of Karna

This episode is devoted to the classic scene of the *Mahabharata* in which Krishna reveals to Karna his true descent. He never was the Son of a Suta, which everyone called him with scorn. No, he was in fact the eldest of the Pandavas-- the original Partha. Now that the truth was out, all Karna needed to do was embrace his Dharma, join his brothers, and assume the title of King of India.

Poor Karna is always the victim of bad timing. It was way too late for such an offer. Perhaps if Kunti had stood up and claimed him as her son during the Pandavas' first military exhibition, he might have come around then, but now there was too much water under the bridge. Karna had been tossed out as a baby like the day's garbage, and had been scorned as a Suta when he tried to display his Kshatriya nature. His modest Suta parents and the evil Kauravas had been the only ones to come to his aid, and he would never give them up.

Krishna failed in turning Karna, but somehow he allowed Sanjay to know of the entire conversation, so the story of Karna's descent and temptation was made known to all the Kauravas. Kunti caught wind of the encounter, and she made a go at turning him. She also failed, but she at least got the promise that he would spare her other sons, and should Arjun die, Karna would take his place as her fifth son.

Being just a story for many, the Sanskrit epic Mahabharat, is pervaded by moments of grave ethical choices; from Draupadi humiliated at Kaurava court, to Arjuna on the battlefield, to Yudhishthira at the gates of heaven, the epic is constantly posing serious ethical dilemmas about the very systems that it itself seems to propose. But the beauty of Karna lies in the fact that how he handles all such situations and acted in ethical way so as to preserve his dignity though siding the evil. This topic will focus on the choice that Karna makes when he is asked by both Krishna and Kunti to fight for the Pandava side. It can be argued that Karna is indeed facing a deep ethical dilemma and that his ethics is existential and not martial. Karna's loyalty to his family and friends is not a simple and straightforward clinging but rather a paradoxical faith that seems to rise above both mere instinctual emotions and systematized ethics. How beautifully he deals with the moral and ethical dilemmas is worthy of the praise. Karna is whole of the epic remains loyal to those who have loved him and still love him. Their love for him both justifies and demands Karna's loyalty. His choice is startling in the context of dharma as 'code for conduct' (as discussed earlier), and the options that dharma provides to an individual (Varna and Jati etc). By examining these options we can see how through the story of Karna's choice, the epic, both undermines the claim of completeness of any human knowledge-system about dharma, and extend the range of what dharma can encompass.

Background Story

On the eve of the great war over the kingdom of Bharata, a god in the form of a manapproaches a warrior preparing for battle. The god is Krisna, an incarnation of Vishnu, and ostensibly the foremost divine presence in the book. And the warrior is Karna, who will fight – and die – on the losing side of the war. Karna is aware that Krisna is a god for Krishna's mortal disguise is a thin veil. We should keep this in mind as we examine Karna's response to krishna's request. First, though, I will begin by introducing Karna through his story as seen from his point of view. Karna is the son of a charioteer couple, and thus, in the social system of the epic, a suta, a member of one of the lower castes of society. Crucially, Karna is not a member, by dint of his parents, of the the aristocratic warrior class (Kshatriya varna). Moreover, the suta jati that Karna does belong to is not merely low, it is an 'against the grain' (pratiloma) jati, that is, it is a jati 'originating' from the (hypogamous) union of a brahmin woman and a kshatriya man. A suta is not just not low, he is an outcast (apasada) and should, in the words of Manu, "make his living by an activity reviled by the twice-born [the Brahmins, the Kshatriyas, and the vaisyas]." Nevertheless, at the same time, the suta jati is also traditionally the jati of the epic reciters, and Krishna himself participates in the epic battle as a charioteer. (Below I will discuss further the implications of Karna belonging to the suta jati.)

As a young man, Karna develops incredible military skills. At one point, he enters a military tournament, a festival intended to celebrate the end of the military training of the Pandava and Kaurava princes. The tournament has proceeded quite far when Karna arrives; in fact, the champion of the tournament, Arjuna, is about to be crowned. Just before the final ceremonies, karna enters the arena and his very presence causes a stir. Karna then reduplicates all of Arjuna's feats one by one. There is one thing left then, to challenge and defeat Arjuna in one-on-one combat. But as Arjuna and Karna prepare to fight, the plot takes another twist and class enters the picture.

Krpa, an instructor of the princes, asks Krna, "what is your kshatriya lineage?" Karna can only hang his head. Then, in another surprising turn, Duryodhana, the eldest of the Kaurava brothers, steps forward and makes Karna a Kshatriya. Citing scripture legalistically, Duryodhana reminds the crowd that **class is not always a matter of birth**. A man who rules a kingdom becomes *de facto* a ksatriya. So Duryodhana bestows a small province on Karna. Immediately, priests are summoned and Karna is anointed. And now that Karna is a Kshatriya, no one can object to the battle between Karna and Arjuna.

At just that moment, Karna's father, the charioteer Adhiratha, enters the arena. And Karna, without hesitation, bows down to his father to show him respect. And this causes a pandemonium both among the contestants and the crowd – there are jeering comments at Karna, there are cries of support – but the net result is that the tournament breaks down and the battle between Arjuna and Karna is postponed. (This will be revisited when I will discuss caste and class issues of Karna's life)

Karna never forgives the Pandavas for the taunts, and, in the years that follow, Karna's anger and envy at the Pandavas only deepens and grows- One interesting example is the princess Draupadi's groom-choice ceremony (swayamvara). Just as at the tournament, Karna is disallowed from even participating. The contest involves stringing a bow and when Karna steps up to try, Draupadi objects, saying that she should not be married to the son of a suta. (Draupadi is a kshatriya princess.) That certainly offends Karna, but the insult is compounded when Draupadi allows a Brahmin attending the swayamvara to compete for her hand. The same argument based on class should indeed apply just as well to the brahmin: as Manu says, "a twice-born man should marry a wife who is of the same class." And even though "marrying up" (hypergqmy) is not disallowed by the dharmashastras (for example by Manu), in theory Draupadi should be choosing among kyatriya princes. In that sense, Draupadi is not acting wrongly, only unconventionally when she allows the Brahmin to compete. To Karna, Draupadi's unfairness lies in the way that she emphasizes convention when it comes to prohibiting Karna from the tournament, but she stretches convention when she allows the Brahmin to attempt to string the bow. The Brahmin turns out to be Arjuna in disguise, and so Draupadi does indeed wind up marrying a ksatriya. To Karna, however, the process that led to that outcome was inconsistent and unfair." (later during game of chess when Yudhisthira lost everything, Karna in revenge points that, since wife is also called Ardhangini, better half of a man, Yudhisthira still possess something to play, and later it turns out to the be one of the causes of the war). As such events harden Karna's anger and envy; it becomes his life's goal to defeat Arjuna. This brings us to the point where Krishna approaches Karna just before the war.

Krishna to Karna

Krishna, the master strategist of the Pandavas, realized that victory was going to be difficult with Karna on the opposite side. After the failure of his final peace mission at the Kaurava court, he takes Karna aside and makes a desperate bid to win him over. He reveals to him the secret of his royal birth. As Kunti's son, Krishna tells him, Karna is the eldest Pandava. If he crosses over, he will be king. Yudhisthira, the crown prince, will stand behind him holding the royal fan; Bhima will hold his 'great white umbrella'; all Pandava allies, kings and their nobel sons, will pay tribute and touch his feet. Listing the long pageant that will follow his train, Krishna proclaims:

> "Let the Pandavas sound out Karna's triumph!, Surrounded by princes, you will be the moon with its stations"

It is a tempting offer. Although Duryodhana had crowned Karna king of Anga, he had in reality remained Duryodhana's retainer; he was never treated as Kshatriya, nor allowed to marry one. Knowing Karna's weakness for Draupadi, Krishna lures him also with the prospect of enjoying Draupadi- He will share her as a wife with his brothers.

"Draupadi will in time approach you"

But Karna, to his great credit, refuses to switch sides. Karna tells Krishna that his loyalty is to Duryodhana, who was there when he needed him. And it is not just a matter of loyalty—it is a question of his word, which he has given publicly. It would be a breach of dharma if he now joined the other camp. 'I cannot act in an untruthful way against the wise son of Dhritarashtra's,' he says. Karna goes on to explain that Kunti, his natural mother, abandoned him as though he were inauspicious, while Radha, the charioteer's wife, brought him up. Hence, Radha is his true mother and Adhiratha his true father. True parentage comes from affection and not from birth. In parting, Karna asks Krishna to keep his identity a secret from the Pandavas. If a principled man, like Yudhishthira, were to find out, he would immediately surrender the realm to his older brother. And he, Karna, in turn, would be forced to pass it on to Duryodhana. Therefore, 'Let conscientious Yudhishthira be king forever,' he tells Krishna.

Some of us who have read the epic do not give him credit for his nobility of character, but see in this act Karna's stubborn refusal to acknowledge Krishna's divinity. But I will discuss this in detail when I will deal with Karna and his loyalty. Yet I would add that Karna ends the dialogue by hugging Krishna and saying that they shall next meet in heaven.

Krishna's efforts are only the first attempt to bring karna to the other side. The second, and perhaps more dramatic attempt, is made by Kunti, Karna's biological mother.

Kunti to Karna

She goes to look for Karna and finds him praying on the banks of the Ganges. As she waits in the shadow of his tall frame, he opens his eyes and greets her with folded hands. 'I am Karna, the son of Radha and Adhiratha,' he says. She tells him, no—he is her son, who came into the world 'as a divine child surrounded by beauty, with earrings and armour'. He should return to his real family and join his brothers. If you and Arjuna are united nothing would be impossible in the world. The Kauravas would be defeated, the realm that has been expanded with Arjuna's valour would be regained and Karna would gain for himself the splendour that was Yudhishthira's, Kunti says. But the way she puts it, particularly in the importance she gives to Arjuna's role in expanding the kingdom and to Yudhishthira's status as its sovereign, reveals her unconscious mind. Karna feels that she still places Yudhishthira and Arjuna above him. Suffering from anxiety about his status and thus sensitive to these nuances, he finds Kunti's desire to get him back functionally motivated and not driven by affection. Even an appeal from his father, the sun god Surya, who instructs him to 'obey his mother's wishes', does not make him waver. In reply, Karna addresses Kunti, not as 'mother', but formally as 'kshatriya lady', a deliberate gesture on his part to make a point about his low status. He tells her politely that he was abandoned by her; so how could he be expected to have sympathy for her as a mother? Worse, being abandoned meant that he was denied fame and glory. Bitterly, he adds:

> I was born a kshatriya, but never received what was due to a Kshatriya What enemy would do anything so evil!

He cannot cross over now, he says politely. It would imply that he had joined Arjuna and Krishna out of fear. If he deserts his friends and allies, they would not think of him as a 'genuine kshatriya'. Besides, he says, true dharma consists in respecting the bonds with those who care and nurture you rather than mere bonds of blood. In a parting gesture, he promises Kunti with bitter graciousness that he will not slay any of the Pandavabrothers except Arjuna. She will thus always have her five sons. If he falls there will be Arjuna, and if Arjuna falls he will be there. Thus mother and son part, with Kunti trembling with grief. The next time she sees her son, Karna is lying dead on the battlefield at Kurukshetra. When Karna told his mother that his 'real parents' were the low caste family who had brought him up and not his royal family to which he had been born, he was in effect rejecting the claim that status arises from birth. In the feudal culture of the *Mahabharata* this must have taken great courage. Moreover, to stand up to his mother and resist her entreaties was also a daring act in a society where one's parents' wishes are almost sacred. Even more admirable, Karna showed a commitment to his word and to Duryodhana. In the end, principle triumphed over his hunger for status. In making this unselfish choice he holds up to the audience an admirable sense of dharma. Karna's search for his identity reminds one of the terrible mistake that society makes in forcing individuals to privilege one identity over all the others. Karna has many identities: he is a caring son, an outstanding warrior, a father, a husband, an extremely generous person, a loyal friend of Duryodhana's. Why must his father's background trump his many rich—perhaps, far richer—identities and become the sole basis of his status in society?

11. Book V: The Book of Effort

The Book of the Effort or Udyogaparva is more or less directly concerned with the preparations for the Great War. This "effort," in Sanskrit *udyoga*, may be understood both as a peace effort, and as a war effort. It also has the meaning "the yoking up" of the horses, chariots, and elephants of the army in preparation for making an attack, also simply yoga, "the yoking".

The structure of this Parva is quite simple: it is the narrative of the negotiations between the Pandavas, who demand their half kingdom back, and Duryodhana, who refuses. These negotiations are formally carried out by means of four embassies, each preceded by a great deal of internal consultation on both sides. Before the negotiations start, each side raises armies, the Pandavas seven, the Kauravas eleven, and thus both are able to negotiate from strength (***Senodyoga Parva***).

Yudhishthira begins with sending a Brahmin, the house priest of his father-in-law king Drupada of Panchala, to Kauravas in order to find out what Duryodhana's attitude is. Before Duryodhana himself speaks up, his father Dhritarashtra decides to send his confidante and charioteer Sanjaya as envoy to Yudhishthira for the double purpose of making a courtesy call – after all, his nephews the pandavas have been gone for thirteen years – and finding out what Yudhishthira's demands really are. While remaining a model of courtesy, the Pandava insists on his kingdom (***Sanjayayana Parva***). Before he hears Sanjaya's report, Dhritarashtraspends a sleepless night, during which he is much edified with a sermon by his brother Vidura (***Prajagara Parva***) and the seer Sanatsujata (***Sanatsujata Parva***).

In the consultations ensuing from Sanjaya's report, Duryodhana is put under great family pressure, but remains adamant, refusing to allow as much as a "pinprick of land" to Yudhishthira (***Yanasandhi Parva***). Before his position has been officially reported, Krishna betakes himself on a peace-seeking mission on behalf of both the parties, but he fails to sway Duryodhana (***Bhagavadyana Parva***). As a last resort, Krishna seeks to win over Karna by revealing his real parentage; his now-revealed mother Kunti tries the same; both fail. Krishna reports to Yudhishthira, who, with many misgivings, orders "the Yoke" (***Karnaupanivada Parva***), and marches out (***Sainyaniryana Parva***). Duryodhana installs Bhishma as marshal of his eleven armies (***Bhishmabhishechana Parva***), and sends Uluka, Shakuni's son, with a declaration of war (***Uluka-Dutagamana Parva***). The Udyoga Parva ends with a review of the principal warriors (***Rathatirathasankhya Parva***), and a lengthy account by Bhishma of the complex pre-history of one warrior, Shikhandi, whom he shall refuse to fight (***Ambopakhyana Parva***), presaging the next Maha Parva, Bhishma Parva, the Book of Bhishma.

Of the eighteen parvas of the *Mahabharata*, Udyogaparva is the fifth one. This has 10 adhyayas and 6682 verses.

1. Senodyogaparva

This upaparva of the Udyogaparva consists of 19 chapters. The Pandavas and their associates felt happy as the marriage of Abhimanyu and Uttara was celebrated. On the second day, the Pandavas were present in the royal court. The old and honourable Virata and Drupada took their seats first in the assembly. Following them, Vasudeva and his sons Krishna and Balarama were seated. The other members included the sons of Drupada, Virata and Draupadi, and other great chariot-warriors. Every one was eager to listen to the words of wisdom of Krishna. The latter started by describing how Sakuni of Sabala defeated Yudhishthira by deceit in the game of dice and grabbed his kingdom. The condition put in the game was that the defeated should go to woods for twelve years and live incognito for one year. The Pandavas who were defeated in gambling stayed in the woods for twelve years and lived in disguise in the kingdom of Virata for one year experiencing many hardships. Because of the treachery of the Kauravas, the Pandavas had to face difficulties. The Pandavas having completed the stay in the woods and the stay in disguise then were asking for their wealth. The truthful Yudhishthira was present there before them along with his brothers. If the Kauravas were to behave offensively with them, the Pandavas would kill them. What was in the mind of Duryodhana, they were not aware of so far. So a virtuous person should go there as an emissary and advise Duryodhana to give half the kingdom to Yudhishthira. Balarama appreciated the speech of Krishana and said that the pious Yudhishthira was in fact asking for only half of the kingdom, foregoing his right over his kingdom. It would be appropriate to send him to Dhritarashtra as a messenger. Lord Krishna gave his consent to that and went away to Dwaraka. Later, the king of Panchala, with the permission of Dharmaraja, decided to send his priest to the Kauravas as an emissary during the auspicious time of Jaya coinciding with the Pushya star. At the command of king Drupada, a Brahmin priest, rich in good customs started for Hastinapura. After sending the Purohita to Hastinapura, the Pandavas decided to send messengers to other kings also. Having done so, Arjuna himself set out for Dwaraka. Duryodhana received information regarding the activities of the Pandavas through his spies. On the same day on which Arjuna reached Dwaraka, Duryodhana also reached there. Both of them went into the chambers where Krishna was asleep. Duryodhana entered first and sat on the high seat at the head side of the bed. Later Arjuna went in and stood at the other side folding his hands in respect. On waking up, Krishna saw Arjuna first. He welcomed both of them and then enquired the reason of their visit. Then Duryodhana requested Krishna's help in the forthcoming war. Then Krishna said that even though Duryodhana had come first, he saw Arjuna first. So he was prepared to help both of them. But according to the word of the scriptures, the younger Arjuna would have the right to choose first his desired object. He had with an army consisting of ten crore Gopa soldiers. They were always prepared for war. On the other hand, he was there all alone. He would neither participate in the war nor hold any weapon. He asked Arjuna to choose one of the two. When Krishna thus offered a choice, Arjuna selected Krishna. Duryodhana who was very much pleased inwardly, chose the whole army. Having thus gained the troops, he went to Balarama and told him the reason for his arrival. Balarama announced that he would support neither Duryodhana nor Arjuna. He advised them to fight according to the rules of war. Duryodhana was pleased within himself, and thought that they would win the battle as Krishna was weakened. Then he went to Kritavarman, who presented him an army of one akshauhini. Duryodhana returned to Hastina satisfied. At the request of Arjuna, Krishna became his charioteer. On receiving the message of the Pandavas, king Salya set out accompanied by his son and a large army to meet Dharmaraja. Having come to know of this, Duryodhana made preparations to receive him half the way. Salya felt very happy and told Duryodhana to ask for a boon. The latter requested him to be the commander of his whole army. Salya accepted it happily. Then he went to Yudhishthira and reported to him about the boon given to Salya. Then Yudhishthira praised him saying that he was equal to Krishna in driving a chariot. And he requested him to help Arjuna if he wanted to do good to him. When Karna and Arjuna would face each other, he should discourage

Karna. Salya agreed to it and said that he would do accordingly. As Fate is powerful, even noble persons would face difficulties now and then. Having said so, he narrated how Indra faced troubles. Then taking leave of him, Salya, the king of the Madras went Duryodhana along with his army. All those kings who were on the side of Duryodhana sent their armies to Duryodhana. Thus the total strength of Duryodhana's army became eleven akshauhinis.

2. *Sanjayayanaparva*

There are 13 chapters in this section. The priest of Drupada went to the Kauravas as an emissary and was warmly received by Dhritarashtra, Bhishma and Vidura. He described the strength and capabilities of the Pandavas and asked the people around to give half of the kingdom to the Pandavas as it was to be bestowed to them rightfully. Bhishma also supported him and started to describe the valour of Arjuna. Interrupting him in the middle, ridiculing his speech, Karna said that Duryodhana would never share, even one fourth of his kingdom with any one out of fear, leave alone half of it. Foolishly Bhishma was turning his mind towards the negative way. Rejecting the words of Karna, Bhishma again eulogized the valour of Arjuna, and referred to the defeat of six great warriors at the hands of Arjuna during the battle at the city of Virata. Then Dhritarashtra reprimanded Karna and revered Bhishma. He said that the advice of Bhishma was beneficial to all. Then he honoured the priest, and having sent him away, decided to send Sanjaya to the Pandavas. At the command of king Dhritarashtra, in order to enquire the welfare of the Pandavas on behalf of the king, and to act in the interest of the family of Bharata, Sanjaya went to Upaplavya to meet the Pandavas. Having met Yudhishthira he enquired his well being. After that Yudhishthira questioned about the actions of the Kauravas. Having answered him, Sanjaya conveyed the message of Dhritarashtra. At that moment, Sri Krishna, Satyaki, king Virata, and all the Pandavas were present there. Sanjaya said that Dhritarashtra wanted peace. He wished that the Pandavas would accept the king's advice, and a treaty could be made between the two camps. Then Yudhishthira remarked that they also did not raise the topic of war. He wondered why the Kauravas were getting nervous. It was Dhritarashtra and his sons who took the path of adharma. The uncouth behaviour of the Kauravas towards them could not be concealed. He demanded that Duryodhana should return the Indraprastha kingdom of the Pandavas. Sanjaya then again spoke about the demerits of the war, and advised Yudhishthira to turn away from it. He further instructed him to distribute all his wealth to his counselors, if at all he was thinking in terms of war at their suggestion, and warned him not to move away from the path of dharma by killing his family members. On hearing that Yudhishthira asked him to decide first whether the Pandavas were in the path of dharma or adharma. Sri Krishna, the lord of dharma, the master of polity was present there. He was a well wisher to both the sides. So he should speak out his mind in that regard. Then Krishna said that he indeed wished the good of both the sides. The Pandavas should make peace with the Kauravas and live calmly. But that would not happen without first appropriating the share of the Pandavas in the ancestral property. The virtuous Pandavas were set for peace; nevertheless they were well equipped for war also. So the facts must be told to Dhritarashtra after proper deliberation. When Krishna said so, Sanjaya took permission to take leave of them and go back to Hastinapura. Yudhishthira then asked Sanjaya to enquire the welfare of all there and report theirs also to them. Then he wanted him to convey the message that the Pandavas were capable of making both peace and war. Sanjaya went to Dhritarashtra with the message and after conveying the welfare of the Pandavas, criticized the deeds of Dhritarashtra. He said that in the whole world that it was only Dhritarashtra who supported his sons in gambling, and praised them. He could then witness the terrible consequences of that. He punished the trustworthy by uniting the untrustworthy. He then said that as he was exhausted, he would convey the message of Yudhishthira in front of every one in the assembly the next day. Dhritarashtra permitted him to go to his house.

3. Prajagaraparva

There are 8 chapters in this section. After Sanjaya left, Dhritarashtra called Vidura. The latter met him as was ordered. The king mentioned the arrival of Sanjaya and said that the latter carrued the message of Dharmaraja to him and went home having criticized him. He would convey the message in the assembly also the next day. The king's heart burned as he did not know what was in the mind of Dharmaraja. Agitated he was, he could not even sleep. He was not tranquil also. He was very much disconcerted. So he requested Vidura to advise him what was good for him. In reply to him Vidura said that sleep will not visit a weak person who opposes a stronger one, or one who has lost all his wealth, or a lustful one or a thief. He then queried whether the king found himself in one of those kinds. Then Dhritarashtra beseeched him to speak some the righteous and the beneficial words. Then Vidura explained about the natures of the knowledgeable and the ignoramus, and advised him on the greatness of the righteous way. At the end he remarked that the five sons of Pandu were like five Indras in capabilities. He further advised him to give kingdom to the Pandavas in the rightful manner, and be happy with his sons. Then Dhritarashtra sought advice on what he should do. Then Vidura again discoursed on the way of dharma. But Dhritarashtra said that he was not satisfied with those words. Vidura then suggested acting amicably with both the Kauravas and the Pandavas. Further, he narrated the argument occurred between Sudhanvan and Virochana for possessing the extraordinarily beautiful Kesini in the swayamavara. He queried how he could desire prosperity while placing the burden of the kingdom on Duryodhana, Sakuni, the stupid Dussasana, and Karna. The Pandavas treated him as a father. He also should treat them as his children and behave accordingly. Asked by Dhritarashtra, he gave an account of the characteristics of a noble born. On hearing it, Dhritarashtra said that Yudhishthira was cheated. So the angry Pandavas would fight with his sons and kill them. That was the reason why his mind was restless. And he requested him to show him the tranquil way. Vidura again advised him to make peace with the Pandavas and prevent Duryodhana from misbehaviour. Dhritarashtra consented with him saying that he also thought so. He had affectionate feelings towards the Pandavas. But his mind turns the other way when he was under the influence of Duryodhana. Nobody can overcome fate. He also considered fate unalterable. The efforts of man are in vain before that.

4. Sanatsujataparva

There are 6 chapters in this sections. Dhritarashtra asked Vidura to tell him if there was anything more to be told. Vidura answered that Sanatsujata, the celebrated son of Brahma alone could clear all the doubts that were in the mind of the king. Having said so, he thought of the sage. After welcoming the sage, who appeared just by thinking about him, Vidura requested the sage, who took rest, to clear the doubts of Dhritarashtra. Dhritarashtra asked the sage whereas according to the latter's theory that there was no death; he however heard that the gods and the demons observed celibacy in order to escape from death. Which of these two was true? Then the sage replied that both the propositions were true. Carelessness is death and carefulness is immortality. The demons were defeated because of their carelessness whereas the gods became equal to the Brahma because they were vigilant. There is no form for the death to see. After dying, man takes birth again to experience the results of his deeds. He cannot transcend death. Thus Sanatsujata explained to Dhritarashtra. And this is called Sanatsujatiya.

5. Yanasandhiparva

This section contains 25 chapters. The next day many kings attended eagerly the assembly to listen from the mouth of Sanjaya the message of the Pandavas. Duryodhana, Dussasana and others were also present. Asked by

Dhritarashtra, Sanjaya started with the message of Arjuna. Whatever Arjuna said, Duryodhana should hear. If Duryodhana would not leave the kingdom of Yudhishthira, he would have to face the consequences. He had to fight with warriors like Bhima, Arjuna etc. Then Duryodhana would repent. Lord Krishna was on their side. Even if Krishna would not participate in the battle, still whose victory the Lord desired in his mind, that person would defeat all his enemies. And Arjuna would win the whole of the country of the Kurus by killing all the sons of Dhritarashtra including Karna. He would not leave any one of the sons of Dhritarashtra. But still, whatever Grandfather Bhishma, Kripa, Drona, Aswatthama and Vidura said would prevail. Let all the Kauravas live for long. Bhishma told Duryodhana that Krishna and Arjuna were the incarnations of Sages Nara and Narayana. For the welfare of the worlds, whenever and wherever the necessity of war occurs, they will take their birth then and there many a time. He warned Duryodhana that if the latter would not listen to his words, then the destruction of the Kauravas was certain. He condemned Duryodhana for agreeing with the ideas of Karna, the son of a charioteer, Sakuni and the evil minded Dussasana. On listening to those words, Karna abused Bhishma and said that he never indulged in anything unpleasant to Duryodhana. Talking about peace with the Pandavas was improper. And he further asserted that he was able to rout the Pandavas all alone. Bhishma reviled the speech of Karna. Drona also supported him and advised to make peace with the Pandavas. Even though the words of Bhishma and Drona were meaningful, Dhritarashtra rejected them and asked again Sanjaya about the Pandavas. Then Sanjaya spoke about them whom Yudhishthira was contacting for help in the war. Dhritarashtra then became terrified on thinking about the prowess of Bhima and Arjuna, and put forth before the Kauravas the matter of making peace with the Pandavas. Sanjaya then recounted the mistakes of Dhritarashtra and advised him to keep on tight leash the evil Duryodhana and his accomplices. Then Duryodhana reassured his father by praising the valour of Bhishma, Drona, Kripa, Aswatthama, Karna and others who were on their side. He said that the Pandavas had only seven akshauhinis. So there was no question of his defeat. He asked his father not to get worried. Then he asked Sanjaya about the preparations for war being done by Yudhishthira and Sanjaya told him everything. Dhritarashtra advised Duryodhana to make peace with the Pandavas. He asked his son to turn away from war. He further advised him to give the rightful share of the kingdom to the Pandavas. Half the kingdom was enough for him to lead his life along with his counsellors. In fact it was Sakuni who was making them do that all. But Duryodhana did not accept his words. He said that he did not invite the Pandavas for a fight placing his confidence on Bhishma, Drona and others. Karna and he had taken the vow to perform the sacrifice of war making Yudhishthira the sacrificial lamb. The chariot would become the altar in that sacrifice. Sword and mace were the sacrificial ladles sruk and sruva. The armour was the deer-skin. The four horses were the four fires. Arrows were the holy grass kusa and fame was the oblation. Karna, Sakuni and he, the three of them would annihilate the enemies. Living with the Pandavas was never possible. He would not give up to the Pandavas even that much of land on which the sharp end of a needle could stand. On listening to those words Dhritarashtra spoke of abandoning his son and again asked Sanjaya to tell about the messages of Arjuna and Krishna. Then Sanjaya reported whatever Krishna had spoken about the valour of Arjuna. Having heard all that Dhritarashtra remarked that the Pandavas were more powerful than the Kauravas. Getting angry at that, Duryodhana boasted about himself. Karna egoistically spoke that he could single handedly kill all the Pandavas. When Bhishma condemned him, Karna left the assembly and went away. Vidura referred to the story of the birds and said that family feud was harmful and advised to make peace with the Pandavas. Dhritarashtra again tried to convince his son. When Duryodhana rejected the proposal of Arjuna and Krishna, then all the kings in the assembly walked out. In the meantime Sage Vyasa arrived there. At his command, Sanjaya eulogized the greatness of Krishna. He said that Krishna was coming to make treaty between the Pandavas and the Kauravas. On hearing that Dhritarashtra felt happy.

6. Bhagavadagamanaparva

This section has 79 chapters. After the departure of Sanjaya, Yudhishthira went to Sri Krishna and sad that they were all safe under his protection. They were challenging Dhritarashtra, Duryodhana and others for a fight. Krishna must save them from the impending war. Because he never coveted kingdom in full. He asked only for five towns. But the wicked Duryodhana was not prepared to give even them also. According to the duties of a Kshatriya, one should fight when there is a wrong doing. Having said so, Yudhishthira sought Krishna's advice on proper way of dealing with the situation. Having listened to him, Sri Krishna spoke of the necessity to go to the Kauravas for making peace for the sake of the welfare of both the Kauravas and the Pandavas. Clearing the doubts of Yudhishthira, he further asserted that he would burn to death all the Kauravas, if at all they misbehaved with him. He must go there whether it would be fruitful or not, in order to escape from the blame. Yudhishthira agreed with Krishna's proposal. Lord Krishna encouraged Yudhishthira for war saying that it was obvious by what transpired so far that war was inevitable. When Bhima spoke in terms of peace, Krishna ridiculed him and encouraged him for war. Bhima explained that it was not out of fear that he put forth the topic of peace. He just did not wish the obliteration of the family of the Bharats. Arjuna, Nakula and Sahadeva also expressed their opinions in that regard. Draupadi articulated before Krishna her mental agony and condemned the talk of peace. With eyes filled with tears she said that if Bhima and Arjuna spoke of peace, becoming cowards, then her aged father with his sons would fight the enemies. She would not be happy and peaceful until she would look at the shoulder of Dussasana cut and lying in the dust. Sri Krishna consoled her. Then in order to accomplish the task of auspiciousness of the Kauravas and the Pandavas, he started for Hastinapura in the favorable time of the star of Revathi named Maitra in the month of Karthika. He explained the good and bad omens during the journey. On his way he comfortably camped at Vrikasthala for the night. Dhritarashtra, who received the news of the arrival of Sri Krishna through his messengers, felt happy, and ordered Duryodhana to make arrangements for welcoming Krishna, and also for constructing rest-houses on the way. Duryodhana made all the arrangements accordingly. However, Krishna did not even cast a glance at them, and directly went to Hastinapura. Dhritarashtra made arrangements to present Krishna many invaluable gifts. Vidura however told Dhritarashtra that Krishna would not accept anything else except water to wash his feet and hands, and enquiries after health. He desired peace between the Kauravas and the Pandavas. Vidura advised Dhritarashtra to obey the words of Krishna. Duryodhana rejected the idea of gifting gold, precious gems etc. to Krishna and declared that he would make Krisna a captive when the latter arrived. When he did so, the whole world would be under his control. On listening to those words of treachery from Duryodhana, Dhritarashtra and his ministers became sad and agitated in mind. Dhritarashtra advised Duryodhana not to like that. Angry at the wickedness of Durodhana, Bhishma walked out of the assembly. The next day Krishna arrived in Hastinapura from Vrikasthala. As he entered the royal court, Dhritarashtra, Drona, Bhishma and others got up from their seats and welcomed him. He then went to the house of Vidura from there. Then he went to Kunti, who was sorrowful, and consoled her. Having taken leave of her, he went to the palace of Duryodhana. Dussasana, Karna and Sakuni were also present there. After welcoming his guest, Duryodhana invited him for lunch. But Sri Krishna did not accept it. When asked about the reason for his refusal, Krishna explained that a messenger can take meals or accept any honour only after accomplishing the task. That is the rule. So he told Duryodhana that he along with his ministers could honour him only after the completion of his job. He told him that it was improper for him and his brothers to fight with the Pandavas without any reason. Whoever hated the Pandavas, hated him also. And whoever was favourable to them was favourable to him. The food which was defiled by the wickedness of Duryodhana was not fit to be eaten by him. Having said thus to Duryodhana, he went to the house of Vidura. He and his followers ate and took rest there only for the night. Then Vidura told Krishna that according to his opinion Krishna's visit was not advisable. Because Duryodhana was of the opinion that Karna alone could defeat all the Pandavas. So he would not accept any treaty. On listening to the words of Vidura, Sri Krishna explained to him the propriety in his efforts for an agreement. The next day Duryodhana and Sakuni came to Sri Krishna, and invited him to the assembly. As soon as Krishna entered the assembly hall, led by the king, Bhishma, Drona and others came forward to worship him. Sages like Narada also came to meet him. After the sage-folk took their seats, Krishna and other royal members took their seats. Later, Krishna looked at Dhritarashtra and said that he came there to seek peace between the Pandavas and the Kauravas so that there would be no killing of the royal warriors. The family of the Kurus was the best among all the royal families. And if any member of that family misbehaved Dhritarashtra should put him on the right track. His son was behaving like a cruel person, abandoning dharma and artha. Making peace between the two sides was in the hands of Dhritarashtra and Krishna. Dhritarashtra should control his son. Krishna would control the Pandavas. Both the sides would be benefited by that. The sons of Kunti were prepared to serve the king. And if necessary, they were prepared for war also. Whatever the king felt good, could be followed. On listening to the words of Krishna, the members of the assembly were astonished, and none could utter a word in answer. Then Parasurama told the story of an emperor Dhambhodbhava and advised Dhritarashtra to make peace. And sage Kanva recounted the anecdote of Matali, the charioteer of Indra, and advised Duryodhana to make peace with the Pandavas. Sage Narada also tried to convince Duryodhana for securing peace, by relating a number of episodes. On the request of Dhritarashtra, Krishna again said explaining to Duryodhana that he should make peace with the Pandavas, and live happily for a long time, having listened to the friends. On hearing such unpalatable words of Krishna, Duryodhana said that Krishna was partial towards the Pandavas. So he was abusing him. All of them, including Dhritarashtra hated him for no reason. But he did not commit any offence. He further declared that even an iota of land would not be given to the Pandavas. That was his decision. Krishna got angry on listening to those words of Duryodhana and having recounted the offences of Duryodhana advised that Duryodhana, Dussasana, Sakuni and Karna should be made captives and handed over to the Pandavas. Dhritarashtra called Gandhari and asked her to convince Duryodhana. Gandhari also advised Duryodhana to take resort to Sri Krishna and make peace with the Pandavas. But Duryodhana did not consider his mother's words also. Duryodhana, Dussasana, Karna and Sakuni secretly conspired among themselves and decided to take Sri Krishna as a prisoner. Satyaki who could understand the mind of others through the gestures they made, grasped the evil plan of the wicked four. He immediately alerted their soldiers at the main gate and gave hint of the scheme of Duryodhana etc. to Sri Krishna. Then he revealed it to Dhritarashtra and Vidura also. At the command of Dhritarashtra, Vidura brought Duryodhana and his brothers to the assembly. Both Dhritarashtra and Vidura again described the greatness of Sri Krishna, and advised him to take the path of virtue. Then Sri Krishna scoffed at Duryodhana for the latter's ignorance in trying to seize him, and showed his Viswarupa. Dhritarashtra, having requested received two invisible eyes from Lord Krishna to watch the Viswarupa. Having known this the sage-folk was astonished and praised the Lord. Later Sri Krishna went to meet his maternal mother Kunti. Sri Krishna reported to Kunti whatever had happened in the court of the Kauravas. Kunti gave her message to the Pandavas at this bidding. On that occasion she narrated the dialogue between the great royal lady Vidula and her son. Later, Krishna after bowing to Kunti, started from there. He took leave of Bhishma and other elders, made Karna get into his chariot, and along with Satyaki went towards the city of Upaplavya. After the departure of Sri Krishna, Bhishma and Drona again tried to convince Duryodhana to make peace with the Pandavas. After leaving Hastinapura along with Karna, Krishna asked him to behave as a brother with the Pandavas. It would benefit him. But Karna expressed his desire of staying on Duryodhana's side. He said that if he gained victory in the battle, they could meet again. Otherwise, they could meet in heaven only. Having said so, he embraced Krishna, and taking leave of him, got down from the backside of the chariot, and getting into his car, returned to Hastinapura. Krishna went to Upaplavya along with Satyaki. Vidura went to Kunti and told her of the impending terrible events between the Kauravas and the Pandavas. The disturbed Kunti met Karna and revealed to him that he was her eldest son, and requested him to side with the Pandavas. But he did not comply with her request and said that he would fight with her sons. But he promised not to kill the other four brothers except Arjuna, even if an opportunity arose to do so. Thus she would be left with five sons even after the battle. They would be five, with Karna if Arjuna was killed and with Arjuna if Karna was killed. Then Kunti and Karna went their way. Sri Krishna on reaching Upaplavya reported verbatim to the Pandavas whatever had happened in the court of the Kauravas and encouraged them for war.

7. Sainyaniryanaparva

There are 9 chapters in this section. Yudhishthira understood from the words of Sri Krishna that the without making a fight Kauravas would not give the Pandavas their share in the kingdom. War was imminent. In the presence of Krishna only he told his brothers that they also heard everything. They had seven akshauhinis of army. Drupada, Virata, Dhrishtadyumna, Sikhandin, Satyaki, Chekitana and Bhima would be the seven commanders for the seven akshauhinis. They had to decide about the Commander in Chief. So they should suggest who had the capabilities to become the chief of the army. On listening to him Sahadeva suggested Virata, Nakula suggested Drupada, Arjuna suggested Dhrishtadyumna, and Bhima recommended Sikhandin as having the required qualifications. Asked by Yudhishthira, Sri Krishna said that Dhrishtadyumna was worthy of becoming the chief of the army. The Pandavas were happy with his suggestion. All the soldiers prepared themselves for war with enthusiasm. Everywhere the sounds of conches and drums reverberated. King Yudhishthira moved in the midst of the army. Along with him went the expert medical team. Draupadi also followed him for a distance and then returned to Upaplavya along with other ladies. Having planned the arrangement of the troops, the army of the Pandavas reached Kurukshetra There was a pious river Hiranvathi of pure waters. On reaching it Sri Krishna got a trench dug and put soldiers on duty to guard it. Thousands of tents were erected separately for the kings to stay. Doctors also stayed there with their equipment. All the material was put in the tents. On the other side, Duryodhana also made his troops set, and ordered the erection of tents. He told the kings to make an announcement that very day to the effect that the troops should march forward for battle the next morning. There should be no delay. Asked by Yudhishthira regarding the appropriate action, Sri Krishna said that the wicked Kauravas were not behaving properly with them. The Pandavas did not want peace with the Kauravas where they had to forego all their wealth. So war with them had to happen. Then Yudhishthira ordered the kings to make preparations for war. King Duryodhana divided his eleven akshauhini army into the best, mediocre and lowly divisions, and placed them at the appropriate places. At Kurukshetra a total of eighteen akshauhinis of army collected together. The eleven commanders of the Kaurava army are Kripacharya, Dronacharya, Aswatthama, Salya, Jayadratha, Sudakshina, Kritavarma, Karna, Bhurisravas, Sakuni and Bahlika. Duryodhana requested Bhishma and made him the commander in chief. Balarama met the Pandavas and having taken leave of them went to worship in the pilgrim centres near the river Saraswati. He did not want to see the annihilation of the family of the Kurus. Dhritarashtra asked Sanjaya about the arrangements of the armies of the Kauravas and the Pandavas. Sanjaya told him to listen to everything.

8. Ulukadutagamanaparva

This section contains 5 chapters. Duryodhana consulted secretly with Karna, Dussasana and Sakuni and decided to send Uluka, the son of Sakuni as a messenger to the Pandavas. He called Uluka privately and asked him to convey the message to the Pandavas in the presence of Sri Krishna only. The message said that the terrific war between the Kurus and the Pandavas had commenced. Whatever oaths the Pandavas took could be fulfilled. Why they were engaging in a sinful action being themselves virtuous men. They asked for only five villages. But Duryodhana knowingly rejected them. The reason was that Duryodhana wanted to make the Pandavas angry somehow to get an opportunity to fight with them. He challenged them to come with Sri Krishna and fight. Then Uluka went to the camp of the Pandavas and met Yudhishthira. He reported to him all that was told by Duryodhana. The irritated Pandavas sent a reply to the message. Sri Krishna also sent a message on his behalf in which he asked Duryodhana to come to the battle field the very next day and give a demonstration of his prowess. Having received that message from Uluka, Duryodhana ordered his army to begin the battle before dawn the next day. Yudhishthira also prepared his troops for battle under the commandery of Dhrishtadyumna.

9. Sthatisthasamkhyanaparva

In this section there are 8 chapters. Having been made the commander in chief, Bhishma told Duryodhana that he had acquaintance with the military arrays of the gods, Gandharvas and the humans. He would mesmerize the Pandavas with that skill. He would fight with the Pandavas while protecting the army of Duryodhana. Thus the mental anguish of Duryodhana should be gone. Then Duryodhana wanted to know the details about the Rathis and Atirathas in his army. Then having described them Bhishma gave an account of the warriors on the side of the Pandavas. He said that Sikhandin was a woman first who later became a man. So he would not fight him. He would kill all other kings who participated in the war, but would never kill the sons of Kunti.

10. Ambopakhyanaparva

There are 24 chapters in this section. Duryodhana asked Bhishma the reason why he would not kill the kings and let them off. Then Bhishma told him the episode of Amba. After the death of his father Santanu, Bhishma keeping his promise crowned his brother Chitrangada. When the latter died, he made his brother Vichitravirya the king. Bhishma decided to bring a suitable girl and marry Vichitravirya to her. He defeated all other kings and brought the three daughters of the king of Kasi Amba, Ambika and Ambalika from the swayamvara hall and sent them to his mother Satyavati to perform the marriage of his brother with them. But Amba, who loved the king of Salva, took permission of Bhishma and went to him. When the king of Salva rejected her, she decided to take revenge on Bhishma who was the prime cause for her misfortune and spent the night in the hermitage of some sages. An old sage Saikhavatya comforted her. Guided by her maternal grandfather Hotravahana, she took refuge with Parasurama. A great battle took place between Parasurama and Bhishma. At the end, Bhishma wanted to use the Prasvapanastra. But at the intervention of Narada, both of them stopped their fight. Princess Amba performed severe penance. By the power of that she became with half of her body a river called Amba, and was born as a girl in Vatsadesa with the other half. Even in that birth also she performed great penance to kill Bhishma. When Siva appeared before her, she asked for the death of Bhishma as a boon. Siva said that her desire would be fulfilled. She was born as a woman, but would become a man some time later. She burnt herself on the funeral pyre on the banks of the river Yamuna in that birth. The childless king Drupada having performed severe austerities sought a son from Siva to take revenge on Bhishma. Then Siva said that the king would get a girl who would later become a man. The queen of Drupada gave birth to a girl. But the king announced that it was a boy. Only Bhishma came to know about Sikhandin through Narada. At the appropriate age Sikhandin's marriage was performed with the princess of the Dasarnas. Having come to know the truth about Sikhandin, Hiranyavarma, the king of the Dasarnas got angry. Sikhandini went into the woods and there requested a yaksha name Sthunakarna a way out from her distress. The yaksha then exchanged his masculinity with her feminity for sometime. Kubera who was annoyed with that cursed the yaksha to continue to be a woman and Sikhandini became a man by the name Sikhandin. As he was a female at first, Bhishma resolved not to kill him in a battle. The armies of the Kauravas and the Pandavas had set out for war.

4
Sudraka's *Mrichchhakatika:* A Contemporary Classic

'Mrichchhakatika' or 'The little clay art' is an ancient Sanskrit play written by king Sudraka(Ujjayini) in 3rd century A.D. *Mrichchhakatika* is one of the most famous prakaranas i.e. a play whose plot is partly derived from history and partly derived from author's fancy of the ancient India. Sudraka had chosen a social theme i.e. love of Charudatta and Vasantasena as the plot for his play, *Mrichchhakatika*. The hero, Charudatta, a middle class man, is a Brahmana youth and Vasantasena, the heroine is an exquisitely beautiful but pure-minded Ganika—courtesan of the same city. The play consist themes of various genres such as romance and comedy while it also deals with an underplot with political overtones.

Sudraka being a Sanskrit writer opens Mrichchhakatika with a benediction, soon after which Sutradhara takes the command of the play in his hand. Another striking thing about the prologue is the information shared by Sutradhara about the death of the author.

The play is set in the ancient city of Ujjayini during the reign of the King Pālaka, near the end of the Pradyota dynasty that made up the first quarter of the fifth century BC. The central story is that of a noble but impoverished young Brahmin, Cārudatta, who falls in love with a wealthy courtesan Vasantasenā. Despite their mutual affection, however, the couple's lives and love are threatened when a vulgar courtier, Samsthānaka, also known as Shakara, begins to aggressively pursue Vasantasenā.

Rife with romance, comedy, intrigue and a political subplot detailing the overthrow of the city's despotic ruler by a shepherd, the play is notable among extant Sanskrit drama for its focus on a fictional scenario rather than on a classical tale or legend. *Mṛcchakaṭika* also departs from traditions enumerated in the Natya Shastra that specify that dramas should focus on the lives of the nobility and instead incorporates a large number of peasant characters who speak a wide range of Prakrit dialects. The story is thought to be derived from an earlier work called *Cārudatta in Poverty* by the playwright Bhāsa, though that work survives only in fragments.

Of all the Sanskrit dramas, *Mṛcchakaṭika* remains one of the most widely celebrated and oft-performed in the West. Unlike other classical plays in Sanskrit, the play does not borrow from epics or mythology. The characters of Śūdraka are drawn from the mundane world. It is peopled with gamblers, courtesans, thieves, and so on. The protagonist of the play, Cārudatta, does not belong to the noble class or royal lineage. Though Vasantasenā is a courtesan, her exemplary attitude and dignified behavior impress the audience. The nobility of the characters does not stem from their social conditioning but from their virtues and behaviour.

Story

Cārudatta is a generous young man who, through his charitable contributions to unlucky friends and the general public welfare, has severely impoverished himself and his family. Though deserted by most of his friends and embarrassed by deteriorating living conditions, he has maintained his reputation in Ujjayini as an honest and upright man with a rare gift of wisdom and many important men continue to seek his counsel.

Though happily married, the recent father of a young son, Rohasena, Cārudatta is enamored of Vasantasenā, a courtesan of great wealth and reputation. At a chance encounter at the temple of Kāma she returns his affection, though the matter is complicated when Vasantasenā finds herself pursued by Samsthānaka, a half-mad brother-in-law of King Pālaka, and his retinue. When the men threaten violence, Vasantasenā flees, seeking safety with Cārudatta. Their love blossoms following the clandestine meeting, and the courtesan entrusts her new lover with a casket of jewelry in an attempt to ensure a future meeting.

Her plan is thwarted, however, when a thief, Sarvilaka, enters Cārudatta's home and steals the jewels in an elaborate scheme to buy the freedom of his lover, Madanikā, who is Vasantasenā's slave and confidant. The courtesan recognizes the jewelry, but she accepts the payment anyway and frees Madanikā to marry. She then attempts to contact Cārudatta and inform him of the situation, but before she can make contact he panics and sends Vasantasenā a rare pearl necklace that had belonged to his wife, a gift in great excess of the value of the stolen jewelry. In recognition of this, Cārudatta's friend, Maitreya, cautions the Brahmin against further association, fearing that Vasantasenā is, at worst, scheming to take from Cārudatta the few possessions he still has and, at best, a good-intentioned bastion of bad luck and disaster.

Refusing to take this advice, Cārudatta makes Vasantasenā his mistress and she eventually meets his young son. During the encounter, the boy is distressed because he has recently enjoyed playing with a friend's toy cart of solid gold and no longer wants his own clay cart that his nurse has made for him. Taking pity on him in his sadness, Vasantasenā fills his little clay cart with her own jewelry, heaping his humble toy with a mound of gold before departing to meet Cārudatta in a park outside the city for a day's outing. There she enters a fine carriage, but soon discovers that she is in a gharry belonging to Samsthānaka, who remains enraged by her previous affront and is madly jealous of the love and favor she shows to Cārudatta. Unable to persuade his henchmen to kill her, Samsthānaka sends his retinue away and proceeds to strangle Vasantasenā and hide her body beneath a pile of leaves. Still seeking vengeance, he promptly accuses Cārudatta of the crime.

Though Cārudatta proclaims his innocence, his presence in the park along with his son's possession of Vasantasenā's jewels implicates the poverty-stricken man, and he is found guilty and condemned to death by King Pālaka. Unbeknownst to all, however, the body identified as Vasantasenā's was actually another woman. Vasantasenā had been revived and befriended by a Buddhist monk who nursed her back to health in a nearby village.

Just as Cārudatta faces execution, Vasantasenā appears and, seeing the excited crowd, intervenes in time to save him from execution and his wife from throwing herself onto the funeral pyre. Together the three declare themselves a family. Reaching the courts, Vasantasenā tells the story of her near death and, following her testimony, Samsthānaka is arrested and the good Prince Āryaka deposes the wicked King Pālaka. His first acts as the newly declared sovereign is to restore Cārudatta's fortune and give him an important position at court. Following this good will, Cārudatta demonstrates in the final act his enduring virtue and charity, appealing to the King for pardon on behalf of Samsthānaka who is subsequently declared free.

Themes

Mrichchhakatika offers the theme of Sudraka being a Kshatriya who was always ready to take advantage of fighting.Mrichchhakatika, which is a ten act play constitutes of various themes making it subject of a talk. Poverty is one of the most central themes of the play. It is the first point of importance that the play makes. Maitreya mentions the days when Charudatta was wealthy, and then he compares it with the days when he is not. Poverty is not simply a social state in which Charudatta finds himself, rather it becomes the very force that derives Charudatta's thought and ideas because in the entire play he is seen coming back to the fact that he is poor; for everything that happens to him, he blames his poor condition.

Another theme that revolves around the play is the theme of love and romance. In the second act, in conversation with her maid Madanika, Vasantsena reveals how she is love sick. Through the theme of love, Vasantsena's boldness is also highlighted when she is seen talking comfortably to her maid about how how she wants to enjoy the pleasure of youth and true love and serve some king who needs to be served for the sake of his money. Vasantsena's love affair also highlights concepts of economic and financial stability. One gets the idea foe the same from the first act when Vasantsena rejects the proposal of King's brother in law and is seen more caring for a poor. This episode throws light on the social contrast that how a woman is supposed to choose a man who is financially stable but rejects him instead. She is well aware of the general pride that men carry with themselves and therfore deposits her ornament with Charudatta.

The character of Sarvilaka is of the thief. Themes of theft and gamble are introduced through this character.Gambling was considered a vice but a legal one. The rules of gambling games were decided by a gaming association. The theft committed by Sarvilaka at Charudatta's house is also important, as it paves the way for the introduction for Charudatta's wife, Dhuta. Also, the play contains references to music, arts and painting suggesting that these things were considered culturally important. Art in the form of music is shown through Rebhila's character, who according to Charudatta is an expert singer. The way Charudatta praises Rebhila, it seems as if he is an ardent lover of arts and music. Further, an act related to money by Charudatta give us an insightful perspective into the relationships of Sudraka's time and the role money played in it. It was the duty of a man to give money and riches to his wife and therefore when woman offers money to her husband, the entire dynamics of the relation is reversed. One gets an idea of the same through Charudatta's speech when he says "Through money, a man becomes a woman; and she who is a woman becomes a man, also through money".

Another important social situation depicted in the play is slavery. It was common for a slave to be bought and sold as if a commodity in a market place.

Society and state in Mrichchhakatika prevailed with full force. Brahmins were seen with great respect and enjoyed certain privileges. Their status in the society also made them immune to the thieves as Sarvilaka says that he would never steal from a Brahmana. Another important thing that the play suggests that Brahmanas also indulged in trade, for the ancestors of Charudatta got rich only after taking to trade.

Yes, Mrichchhakatika is a contemporary classic because it is able to stand the test of the time. There are various instances and situations in the play that makes it a contemporary classic. Set in the city of Ujjayani, it throws light on romance, comedy, and other political aspects. For instance, the character of Dhuta is seen of a chaste, dedicated and a devoted wife who is concerned about the character of her husband. Alike the woman in contemporary times who supports her husband in every aspect of life and praises him, Dhuta's character reveals her dedication towards her husband. She carries the willingness to help her husband at any cost.

Another feature that makes *Mrichchhakatika* a contemporary classic is it's heroic element. Charudatta, being the protagonist of the play shows nobelity in his character. He is a high-minded Brahmin, a man of unbending principle, and self-righteous. He is the one who spends all his fortune in the act of private charity and public utility. It shapes as an example of a perfect classic play where the hero behaves in a responsible way. Characters like him in Sudraka's play, are people who would not be out of place even in modern India. Mrichchhakatika gives a view of urban life. Through this play one can get a glimpse of the ordinary life.

Mrichchhakatika is much celebrated in the West because of its plot structure and also remains prominent drama in Sanskrit, maiking it a contemporary classic even in today's times which is widely translated, adapted and performed internationally.

New Rendering of *Mrcchakatika*

Mrcchakatika translates into English as The Little Clay Cart. There must be something in this play which got eminent Sankritists of our time, like Arthur Ryder and Moreshwar Kale, to name its author in the company of the other three great playwrights. First, it is very good drama and an excellent comedy. Second, its tone and realism give it a more contemporary appeal. The Little Clay Cart is a play rich in humour and tenderness, and crowded with action in quick changing scenes.Its main story, of love between the poor but noble-minded Charudatta and the virtuous courtesan Vasantasena, is interwoven with another of political intrigue leading to the overthrow of a wicked king.

Apart from sensitive romantic interludes, the scenes range from attempted sexual molestation and virtual murder, a court of criminal justice in session and an execution about to take place. The main players are supported by a lively host of lesser characters, chief among whom is the hero's adversary, a remarkable and vivid combination of villain and bufoon. Besides him there are faithful friends and loyal servants of either sex, a gambler-cum-burglar turned Buddhist monk and a revolutionary with his sympathizers. There are also the hero's wife, whose cordial meeting with his inamorata was considered by some critics a contravention of traditional literary norms, and his infant son whose demand for a toy gives the play its name. The modern appeal of *Mrcchakatika* also derives, it must be noted, from its praise and acceptance in the West. According to literary historian Winternitz, while the older Sanskrit works on poetics and criticism did not seem to consider this play important enough for quoting examples from it, in Europe it was well received from the beginning. First publi-shed in Bonn in 1847, its German translations appeared in the subsequent seventies, followed by those in English, French and other European languages, some also enacted on the stage. In the words of Indologist A.L.Basham, 'to a Western audience, it is certainly the most appreciated of Indian plays'. While the masterpieces of Kalidasa and Bhavabhuti drew from Indian mythology, an understanding of which is necessary for the fullest comprehension of their nuances, Sudraka, to quote Ryder, 'has a cosmopolitan character' and his characters are 'citizens of the world'. Ryder's own translation was staged at the University of California's Greek Theatre in 1907, the first ever performance of a Sanskrit play in the USA, of which this year is the centenary. The book under review is a new translation, described as abridged and adapted for the modern English stage. Vidwan Tenneti mentions in his translator's note that the play has been staged in the original Sanskrit, Bengali and Telugu in the recent past. It also featured in Hindi and Telugu on Doordarshan, Delhi and Akashvani, Hyderabad, and has film versions in Kannada and Hindi. An English translation was staged in New York in 1924. His commendable effort is to create a version for modern presentation in English. This is perhaps the only way for making such classics known today. Tenneti states that as the original play contains lengthy descriptions and soliloquies which impede the 'dramatic tempo', he has left out parts of some long passages. In a few places the textual material has also been rearranged for better presentation. However nothing of significance has been omitted. One of the omissions is that of the original prologue, which gives the play's name and the only known details of its author Sudraka. The adaptor has also rendered in prose all the gnomic and descriptive verses, some of great beauty, with which the play's dialogue is interspersed in the traitional manner. However neither detracts from his adaptation in conveying something of the original's pace and tone. But a translation for the stage must eventually be judged by how it reads and sounds. On this score there are some avoidable lapses where archaisms are mixed uncomfortably with contemporary language. Here is an example, the villain Sakara trying to make a pass at the heroine: 'Stop, Vasanthasena, stop. Why dost thou run, dost thou scamper, dost thou flee? Will you die, if you stop for a moment, my beauty? My heart is burning with love for you, like a piece of meat fallen on glowing coals.' Such passages could well inhibit worthwhile directors from considering this version for a production. A.N.D. Haksar is a well-known translator of Sanskrit classics, his latest being Subhashitavali—An Anthology of Comic, Erotic and Other Verse (Penguin, 2007).

5

Shankaradeva's *Parijata Harana*

The tradition of drama in Assam is very old. The people of Assam has been closely connected with drama, since the days of Srimanta Sankardeva (1449-1568). During his time it was not known as drama but bhaona or ankia nat. But that does not mean the people of Assam were entirely deprived of the entertainment of visual arts before drama or bhaona properly emerged. There are various forms of folk arts with dramatic elements even before the birth of Sankardeva. Even to day, these folk performing arts have occupied a special position in the heart of the people of the state.

Sankardeva, who is regarded as the father of Assamese drama drew much inspiration from these indigeneous art forms. Born in 1449 at Alipukhuri near Bordowa, Sankardeva initiated a bhakti movement, known as the Neo-Vaisnavite Movement and brought a spiritual literary and artistic Renaissance in Assam. Differentiating neo-vaisnavism from the rest of the mainstream vaisnavism was to eradicate certain beliefs and practices was Sankardeva's main motive. Practices like animal sacrifice, idol worship is little encouraged in Neo-Vaishnavism. Worshipping anyone but Krishna(human incarnation of Lord Vishnu) is the supreme belief that Sankardeva propogated. 'Idol worship' is another practice that Sankardeva didn't propogate unlike the mainstream hinduism. Neo-Vaishnavism is also known as 'Naam Dharma', 'Naam' refers to 'name' i.e. name of Lord Krishna and 'Dharma' refers Religion. The movement may therefore be called a part of the all India Vaisnavite Movement Sankardeva was a genius, prophet and seer in whom the whole of Assamese culture and tradition may be said to be epitomized. In his long twenty years of pilgrimage Sankardeva had visited almost all the sacred places of Northern India and acquired knowledge to develop the so long dormant Assamese culture and tradition. Sankardeva laid special emphasis on shravan and kirtana that is listening to the name and praising the one and only one supreme Lord by chanting him again and again. His activities especially, his heart searching messages left a deep impression in the heart of the people of Assam. Besides, he was inspired by the Indian classical tradition of drama associated with religion. It is quite possible that Sankardeva must have had a thorough understanding of Sanskrit dramaturgy as envisaged in Natyasastra and at least a first hand knowledge of some of the theatre forms prevailing in some of the regions he came across during his wide range of pilgrimage To preach his neo-vaisnavite religion, Sankardeva innovates a new kind of dram atic, perform ance know n as bhaona or ankia nat. Sankardeva's bhaona is a dramatic composition in a single act depicting the vaisnavite faith. While Sankardeva was only nineteen, he performed his first bhaona - Chihna Jatra, at his birth place Bordowa. In Chinnayatra Sankardeva, the composer and director of the play, played the role of Narayana (Lord Krishna) while Sandhara Doloi and Dhawjaram, the son of Chanderi Budi played the role of Brahma and Har respectively.

Chida the son of Raghupati Rajak; Chand, the son of Bhekuri Hira; Rupai, the son of Nimai Kumar; Sunanda, the son of widowed Mahindri; Kamapur, the son of Narottam Mishra and Bangaya, the brother of Sankardeva played the role of six Lakshmi.

Sankardeva's Plays and its Characteristics

Sankardeva's Parijat Haran, Rukmini Haran and Ram Vijoy are full-fledged plays having definable plots, characters and dialogues like modem play. On the other hand Keligopal and Kaliya Daman may be considered as small plays. While choosing the themes for his plays from the numerous stories of the two epics, The Ramayana and The *Mahabharata* and The Bhagawat Purana, Sankardeva took into consideration the inherent dramatic qualities to amuse as well as to give religious teachings to the people of Assam. He first entertained the audience with a thrilling drama and then brought home the message of complete submission to lord Krishna. 'Sankardeva's ankiya nats have both a sensuous and an intellectual appeal. These plays exercised a tremendous influence on the national and cultural life of Assam; they led to the growth of the popular stage, and development of music and dancing. ' 15 As printing was unknown during Sankardeva's time, the performance of ankiya nat easily won the heart of all classes of spectators. Sankardeva was successful in spreading his Neo Vaisnavite faith among the masses through the performance of Ankiya Nats. Besides, the popularity of Ankiya Nats inspired him for the creation of a new type of narrative poem called Bhatima. It should also be noted that the growth of Ankiya Nat was influenced by the earlier practice of reciting Kavyas and Sastras in social and religious congregations.

Motive

The Sanskrit drama is essentially aristocratic. Unlike the Sanskrit drama,

Sankardeva's Ankiya Nat was essentially for the common people. Through his heart searching knowledge, Sankardeva always tried to give the common men justice and equality. The motto of his Neo-Vaisnavite movement is 'the service to humanity is the service to god'. Sankardeva had always given emphasis in installing the message of bhakti into the hearts of his disciples. So he kept plot, characterization and dialogue in secondary place. He consumed his whole energy towards evoking a devotional fervour in the audience. He did not aim at the originality of plot or at life like characterization. The plot of an ankiya nat is so arranged as to glorify the hero, Krishna or Rama. The characters therefore do not admit realism. They are simple not complex, types, not individuals. There is no place for tragedy in ankia nat as in the Sanskrit drama. It should be noted that all the plays of Sankardeva are taken from the Bhagavata and the Puarana, except the Ram Vijoy, where the story' is based on the Ramayana and has some features resembling to the Mahanataka.

Language

Language in the plays of Sankardeva, we find mainly the use of two languages: Sanskrit and Assamese Brajavali (Old-Assamese). Sanskrit is used normally by Sutradhara in the invocation (nandi). It is also used in the slokas which were interwoven the whole play. There are also some occasional phrases in Sanskrit quite visible in the Assamese portion of the stage directions. Sankardeva used Assamese Brajavali to make the performance intelligible even to the illiterate people and the women belonging to the land.

Stage Performance

During Sankardeva's time there was no theatre or well decorated rabhas. The Satras, Namgharas or the prayer halls located in different villages serve the purpose of stage or rabhas for dramatic performances. These temporary rabhas were in reality a large open pendal furnished with a covering or a canopy (ehandratapa) of ornamented cloths or grass appropriately decorated. The ground is divided into two blocks separated by a wide passage from one end to the other. At the upper end of this marked arena there is a thapana, placed to worship Lord Krishna and at the other end there is a dohar (orchestra) or a place for chorus and musicians (Gayan Bayan). Behind dohar there is a painted curtain (ar-bastra) which takes the place yavanika of the Sanskrit plays. Behind this curtain and often at some distance there is a green room (cho ghara or nepathya ghara). This room is used for make-up and to keep the accessories including bows, arrows, weapons, masks, dress etc. Near the thapanas, carpets (dalicas) are placed specially for distinguished spectators including Gohains & Mahantas. Remaining space is kept for other spectators where special bamboo mats (dharies) are provided. For female spectators separate space nearby the male is arranged A management of light for this performance was unique. A performance was usually held at 9 O' clock at night and it continues till dawn. A special type of candle or lantern of mustered oil; called gasas were used to light up the whole area. Sometimes some movable torches called mahatmas made of bamboo were also used to provide light in the performing arena. To lit up these mahatmas for the whole night a few people were specially recruited. Their chief job was to pour mustered oil in these lanterns for the whole night taking limited intervals. The Actors during Sankardeva's time an actor was called a nartaka or natuwa (dancer). Now-a-days a common word bhaworiya (actor) is also used. The term nartaka or natuwa points to the predominating element of dance in, dramatic representations as a whole and in each individual actor's role in particular; while bhaworiya means one who represents others' character.26 However it should be mentioned that the principal actor in a dramatic performance is undoubtedly the Sutradhara (stage manager). As in Sanskrit drama the expression "iti Sutra niskrantah" (then exit stage manager) occurs at the end of the prologue (prastabvana) of the Assamese plays. In Sanskrit drama after his formal exit the stage manager never enters the stage again and the performance is left to the actors themselves. But in Assamese plays Sutradhar is found present on the stage even after his formal exit at the conclusion of the prologue (prastavana). It should be mentioned that the role of female characters are performed by male as they were not allowed by tradition to take part in dramatic performances. This resulted in poor depiction of the women character on stage.

In Sanskrit drama, no attempt had ever been made to introduce painted scenery. In Assamese drama also, when the system of stage was open from all sides, no permanent background was used. But according to the *Katha Guru Charita* and *Bordova Charit*, Sankardeva painted scenes of seven heaven (sat vaikuntha) on sheets of paper (tula pat) for the first known performance of his play Cinnayatra. The biographers however do not account for Sankardeva's later discarding painted background. For stage paintings they used generally vermilion (hengul), yellow arsenic (haital), indigo chalk (dhal), brown ochre (gereu), lamp black, collyrium, mica etc. These colours were used usually in painting the four walls of Kirtan Ghara or namghara or in ordinary paintings.

Use of effigies and masks were quite common during Sankardeva's time. In Kathaguru Chant it is clearly mentioned how Sankardeva made the effigy of Govardhan hill in the Govardhan Yatra and the effigy of the serpent demon Kaliya in the *Kaliya Daman* and the man in this role entered into it and spoke from within. Besides, elephants, Hanumanta, Garuda and Jambubanta were also made with the help of bamboos and clothes. The use of masks is another striking feature of Assamese acting. Generally a mask is worn over face; sometimes however a mask covers almost the whole body of the wearer. A mask hides the identity of a person and helps to assume the identity of another character. Actors playing the role of gods, asuras, raksasas, monkeys, birds, reptiles, etc. wore various types of masks. As for instance the actor playing the role of Ravana and Brahma wore a mask of ten and four heads respectively to represent these characters. Usually three kinds of masks were used in ankiya nat. These are:

1. O f animals such as garuda, jatayu, kalinag, hanuman etc.
2. Of demons such as those of the ten headed Ravana or other raks has as.
3. Of buffoons or jesters.

The faces of the characters like Krishna, Ramchandra, Narayana, and some others were painted with blue colour. On the other hand characters like the sages and the brahmins were painted with red and rateasas with black colour. However, it was a tradition that nobody without a mask could represent king. And that is why, rows of ready made masks with their names, was kept in store rooms of the satras. Usually, the masks are made of clay, wood or bamboo and clothes and they are painted suitably with lime vermilion (hengul), yellow arsenic (haital), indigo and lamp black. Musical Instruments There are mainly two types of musical instruments used in bhaona performance - the midang (drum) and the tal (cymbal). Midang (in Sanskrit Mrdang) is a membrophonic (Avanddha Vadya) instrument. It is a kind of drum where the two flat ends of which are prepared out of cattle's hide, and which is beaten with fingers and palms of the hands. The body of it is made of dried earth, equipped with tight strings fastened to the two ends. Another membrophonic instrument used in bhaona performance is called khul.

According to Charit puthi, Sankardeva, first made a khul with the help of a kumar (porter) of a village named Kapilamukh. The shell of the portion of it is made of clay and burnt red. The two skin head of this musical instrument are tightened by straps over the body. The right hand top of a khul which is small in size produces rhythmic pitch note, while the left hand top of bigger circular size produces drab or dull sound. It has to be mentioned that the khol is a direct descendent of mridanga, an instrument of pan-Indian currency. The tal or cymbal is a idiophonic instrument (Ghana vadya) made of brass. Two pieces of round brass plates are held in two hands to produce sound. There are different types of taal used in different occasions of Assam. These are kartaal, bhortaal, raamtal, khutital, mandira etc.

During Sankardeva's time the actors wore costumes of various designs representing various characters and these were especially prepared. Usually the male characters wore crown, cap, matted hair, false beard and whiskers suitable to their age and position. Female characters if young tied their false black hair in a single knot and if old or aged false grey hair loose. These characters also wore all kinds of Assamese ornaments appropriate to their age and sex, including tinkling bells (ghugura) and anklets (nepur). The sutradhara wore a peculiar type of white garment - a long flowing gown reaching down the heels, a bodice covering the dust and a high turban or crown on the head. This is also applicable to the chief ministers, though they used a cap in place of turban or crown. Female characters usually put on white gown called mekhela with ornamental coloured bodice. Sages wore tight waist clothes and scarves of pale red (gerua) ascetics rags and Siva a tiger skin.30 Although Sankardeva had developed ankiya nats largely out of the native and indigenous materials, the influence of Sanskrit drama and dramaturgy is also perceptible to a great extent Sankardeva himself calls his dramatic works nata, nataka or yatra in various parts of his plays. But the Charitkars (biographer) in latter period named these plays as ankiya nats.

The main aim of a bhaona performance is to arouse devotion to the Bhagavata religion, not only with sermonizing but through songs, dances, dialogues and different sentiments which may have direct bearings on devotion. However some other sentiments are also dexterously displayed without causing any strain on the main objective. But realization of the rasas (sentiments) to the fullest extent is not pursued in the performance of a bhaona especially in a play by Sankardeva. W henever the audience is at the peak of enjoying a particular sentiment mostly heroic, there comes an interpolation through the Sutradhara. The Sutradhara has a vital role to play throughout the proceeding of the play to remind the audience of the situation. Thus the Sutradhara serves the purpose of alienating the audience's imagination from the theatre and prompts him to realize the truth of devotion. After Sankardeva's death the satras located in different places of Assam played a vital role to popularize Sankardeva's bhaona. The chief f the satra, known as satradhikar took the initiative to perform this art form on some special occasions like Janma Astami i.e. Sankardeva's birth anniversary. The name of some of these satras were - Auniati Satra, Dakshin Pat Satra, Garmur Satra, Kamalabari Satra, Bordova Satra,

Nikamal Satra, Bholaguri Satra and Chaliha Bareghar Satra. During that period the main aim of a bhaona performance was to spread the sacred message of vaisnava religion of Sankardeva. Gradually when the general people started to compose bhaona people felt a sort of extra taste in a bhaona performance, as entertainment became a special concern for these dramatists.

Parijata-harana

Parijata-harana Naat as of Sahkaradeva centre round the theme of'harana' (which means abduction as well as stealing or robbing). Harana' (stealing) of the divine Parijata flower constitutes the theme of the nata bearing the same name. One day celestial sage Narada calls on Krsna to report the evil doings of Narakasura of Pragjyotispura. He has with him a divine Parijata flower which he offers as a present to Krisna telling him about its wondrous virtue. Narada then describes the sad plight of the gods and goddesses of heaven in the hands of demon Naraka and urges upon him to rescue them. Krsna assures Narada of killing Naraka. Then turning towards Rukmini who has been sitting by him, he puts the divine flower in her hair. Mischievous Narada reports this incident in an exaggerated way to Satyabhama, another consort of Krsna's with a view to rouse her jealousy. She in fact smarts from a feeling of humiliation and insists on Krsna bringing a Parijata for herself. Not satisfied with Krsna's promise she accompanies him to heaven. So Krsna takes her with him and after killing Narada arrives heaven and sends Narada to collect a flower called Parijat from Indra. But Saci, the consort of the king of heaven, refuses to give the flower. At this enraged Krsna uproots the whole plant to carry with him and as a result a fierce fighting breaks not between Indra and Krsna. Even Satyabhama and Saci quarrel and there is angry exchange of words between them. In the fighting Indra is defeated and he acknowledges Krsna as the Supreme Lord and presents him the plant of the Parijata flower. Krsna carries it and plants at the gate of Satyabhama's palace.

We know from Sankaradeva's own admission that he had made use of both the Bhagavata and Harivamsa in composing that poem. Some crities therefore try to assert that in case of the play on the same topic Sankaradeva used Harivamsa and Visnu-purana along with the Bhagavata as the source of the play. But neither the plot nor the sequence of events in the nata lends support to this view. Of course in composing Parijata-Harana Nata he exploited both the Bhagavata and Harivamsa for materials. In the Bhagavata both the episodes of killing Narakasura and of stealing the Parijata from heaven are included in the same chapter and Sri Krsna is shown to have accomplished both the aims in a single journey. But in Harivamsa these two episodes are treated separately as two distinct and different episodes. In including both the episodes in his Parijata-Harana Nata, Sankaradeva has definitely adhered to Bhagavata only.

The theme, though borrowed from original Sanskrit scriptures, bear indelible stamp of Sankaradeva's creativity. In the construction of the plot as well as in characterization he has displayed his originality and his skill in the use of dramatic technique. As for instance in the original Sanskrit stories there are no names to the bhatas (mendicant singers). Sankaradeva has given them names and identity in his nata.

In Parijata-harana Nata he added new dimensions to the character of Narada and depicted him as a mischievous person playing tricks for fun. The quarrel between Satyabhama and Sad towards end of the play is also Sankaradeva's own creation which helps in taking story to its climex.

Within the limited scope of his best and dramatically superb play Parijata-harana Nata, Sankaradeva has created a number of memorable characters. Among them the most noteworthy are Krsna, Narada, Indra, Rukmini, Saci, Satyabhama and others.

Sri Krsna: The chief protagonist of this nata also is Sri Krsna. The character displays a unique juxtaposition of divinity with humanity. While in some of his actions he appears human, in others his devine nature is revealed. Narada at one place of the nata aptly observes: Oh! Lord Krsna prjecting yourself as the best of men you have charmed all, they donot know that you are God incarnate; but I know the truth by the strength of my devotion; oh Lord how can you deceive me.

In spite of his divinity he behaves like a man. He is full of humility and revers the elders and the wise as is evident from the respect shown to Narada.

The natas also stress on his amorous nature. His deep feelin go flove towards Rukmini is seen when he presents the Parijat flower, that was offered to him by Narada, to her. But mischievous Narada reports this in an exaggerated manner to another consort of Krisna, Satyabhama to play upon her feeling of envy and vanity. His adventure does not end there. He comes back to Krisna to report that "se priya satyabhama parijataka nimite apamane annapana saba carala '3 (Your darling Satyabhama has stopped taking food and drink out of deep feeling of humiliation for the Parijata). Krsna is moved and rushes to appease her. He assures her of his love and affection and promises to fulfil all her hearts desire.

We also find him as a henpacked husband in his failure; to refuse to ta ke Satyabhama with him in his adventure of collecting the Parijata. It is for her he engages himself in a battle with Indra, the king of gods. But he is shown more as an incarnation of Supreme Lord Visnu when he kills tyrannical Narakasura to relieve the world of the wickeds. He appears as a saviour of men and gods alike. Thus in Krsna we have a dual identity, one as the incarnation of Visnu and the other as a mortal with all the noble virtues.

Narada: Mischievous Narada of Parijata-Harana Nata is a unique creation of Sarikaradeva's genius. He has been the source of the humour of the play. He is depicted as a person who enjoys provoking other people to quarrel. Narada plays the pivotal role in the development of the plot. It is Narada who provokes envy and jealousy of Satyabhama against her coconsort Rukmini. All the actions of the nata are in a wav result of this feeling of envy of Satyabhama provoked by Narada.

Narada is also instrumental in leading Krsna to fight Indra for the Parijata plant, for he gives an exaggerated report about Saci's refusal to part with the Parijata plant.

Comenting on the character of Narada Dr. Harinath Sarmadalai observes that Narada "is worthy of reverence, honourable and a true devotee of the Lord, but also extremely mischievous. He enjoys twisting and distorting reports to make people quarrel. It is in his very nature. But such actions are without any selfish motive. If there is any it is only to show the greatness of God through conflict. It is with such a motive he creates the feeling of envy and resentment in the heart of Satyabhama. The development of the plot entirely owes to this action of Narada".

Indra: Sankaradeva seems not have given much importance to this character in his nata. He is depicted merely as a helpless and weak king. Of course at the beginning of the nata we have a picture of a person who is full of humility and gratitude to Krsna. Tyranny of Narakasura drives him to Krsna and he prays to him -"jagannatha trahi, trahi " (O Lord of the Universe, please deliver me from the crisis). On Krsna s arrival at heaven after the slaying Narakasura Indra receives him with great reverence and with a feeling of humility expresses his gratitude. He says, 'he krsna papi narakasuraka mari hamaka krtartha kayala/ barambara tuhu uddhara karaha/ tohaka guna sujave nahi pari " (Oh! Krsna you have really blessed me by killing Narakasura. You have delivered me again and again. I cannot repay my indebtedness to you).

On the other that very Indra at the behest of consort Saci fights with him for a mere Parijata flower and is vanquished and humiliated. Thus in Indra we do not have a picture of a powerful king appropriate to his position as the king of heaven.

Satyabhama: She the most boastful, envious and arrogant of the eight consorts of Lord Krsna. She is seen sulking like a common woman. She is not appeased even by the sincere promise of Krsna to bring the Parijata flower for her and insists on accompanying him to heaven, lest Krsna may offer the flower to someone else. She in fact says to Krsna: "he swami hamara bahuta satini, ibara parijata ani kona strika dewaba tahe bu jaye nah i, hamu kadacito tohari sanga nahi caraba" (Oh, m y husband, I have a number of co-consorts. I don't know to which of consorts you offer the Parijata this time. I will, therefore, accompany you wherever you go).

Even in the qurrelling/she is involved in an angry exchange of words with Saci. She scolds Saci using vile language like an ordinary rustic woman. Seeing her thus quarrelling Indra tells her that she is the most quarrelsome of all the con sorts of Krsna.

Again after having the Parijata plant for herself she teases Rukmini by addressing her as princess of Bidarbha and scronfully draws her attention to her own good fortune.

Thus, in Satyabhama we have more of a picture of a common village woman than a queen of a kingdom. She seems not at all worthy to be a consort of L ord Krsna

Rukmini: On the other hand in Rukmini-Harana, the daughter of King Bhismaka, we find a picture of feminine beauty, grace and dignity. She is an ideal consort of Lord K rsna. She is amiable in nature and full of humility. A true devotee of Krsna she deems herself fortunate in being able to serve him as his wife. On hearing; the wondrous power of the Parijata flower that is offered to Kr sna by Narada she begs for it with out beinaware that it may arouse envy of Satyabhama. The flower is of no special worth to her as evident from her polite reply to Satyabhama's boastful utterance after having the Parijata plant. According to Rukmini when you have the rarest opportunity in whole Universe to serve the feet of Supreme Lord Krsna which fufils all the purposes of life - dharma, artha, kama and moksa, what value is your Parijata ? Thus she is projected as vain and boastful woman in the nata.

Saci: In Parijata-harana Nata Saci, the conort of Indra, the king of the gods, appears as an ordinary woman of quarrelsome and proud nature. She has been the source of entertainment and humour of the nata. When Narada asks Indra for a Parijata flower for Krsna she promptly replies before her husband could say anything: Indra cannot give my Parijata. This refusal ultimately leads to the battle between Indra and Krsna. She herself becomes engaged in a bitter exchange of angry words with Satyabhama. Infact she instigated Indra to fight by her insinuating comment that her husband is devoid of manly prowess; in the scene of bitter quarrel with Satyabhama she appears more like a common woman than a queen. In narrating the scandals of Krsna and in scolding Satyabhama in vile languages she displays her inferiority of taste. Thus she is projected as vain and boastful woman in the nata.

There are a few more minor characters in the nata like Narakasura, Basumati, Aditi and others, but none of them has any significant contribution to the development of the plot.

The two characters common to both the natas are Sri Krsna and Rukmini. The chief protagonist of both the natas, Sri Krsna is shown as an incarnation of Visnu, the Supreme Lord of Universe. Yet he is bom in this earth as a mortal human being endowed with all noble virtues. We see him as an ardent lover and a great fighter. In Rukmini-Harana Nata hearing the stories of beauty and grace of Rukmini he abducts her and defeats Rukma, Sisupala and others who oppose him. On the other hand in Parijata-harana Nata he is involved in a deadly battle just for a Parijata flower for his dear wife Satyabhama.

In the nata we find Rukmini as an ardent lover with immense fortitude and as a true devotee of Lord Krsna. Amidst dangers and difficulties she does not lose her composure. When she learns that her brother Rukma will not marry her to Krsna, she does not lose her patience and sends Bedanidhi with a letter to Krsna. With deep faith in God she marries Krsna against the will of her brother.

In Parijata-harana Nata, hearing, the virtues of the Parijata flower she gets the flower by humbly begging for it. Again, when Satyabhama boasted of her good fortune in having the entire Parijata plant for herself Rukmini with great humility points out to her that being able to serve Lord Krsna is the joy and achievement of life.

In the play Sankaradeva has shown great dexterity and skill in characterisation. Like modren playwrights he has created characters, complex in temperament and motivation and represented with subtle particularity. According to Dr. Satyendra Nath Sarma: "Parijata-harana Nata can be called the best from the point of view of dramatic technique. Generally dialogues and characterization are not given much importance in the Ankiya natas. But in composing Parijata-harana, the saint seemed to have particularly careful about these two elements of drama. As a drama undoubtedly Parijata-harana is his best nata." But the prime objective of the natas has been to inculcate Vaisnava concepts of religion and to make the untutored masses vicariously participate in the emotions and the convictions of the characters of the natas about the greatness of Krsna worship cult.

6

Ilango Adigal's *The Book of Banci*: The Tale of an Anklet

Ilango Adigal was a Tamil poet and a Jain monk, who was instrumental in the creation of Silappathikaram, one of the five great epics of Tamil Literature. Prince Ilango was the brother of Chera king Cheran Chenguttuvan (in modern day Kerala), in South India. Ilango Adigal was born in the Chera dynasty that ruled parts of what is now known as Kerala, but formed part of the Tamil Land. According to a legend, an astrologer predicted that he would become the ruler of the land and to obviate such a happening, especially when his elder brother the rightful heir was alive, the prince became a Jain monk taking the name of Ilango Adigal, Adigal indicating that he had became a Jain monk.

The Tale Of An Anklet or ***Silappadikaram*** is one of Five Great Epics according to later Tamil literary tradition. Ascetic-prince Ilango Adigal is credited with this work, who was the younger brother of reputed warrior-king Senguttuvan of the Chera dynasty.

As a literary work, Silappadikaram is held in high regard by the Tamil people. It contains three chapters and a total of 5270 lines of poetry. The epic revolves around Kannagi, who having lost her husband to a miscarriage of justice at the court of the Pandyan Dynasty, wreaks her revenge on his kingdom.

Regarded as one of the great works of Tamil literature, the Silappadikaram is a poetic rendition with details of Tamil culture; its varied religions; its town plans and city types; the mingling of different people; and the arts of dance and music.

Silappadikaram has been dated to likely belong to the beginning of Common era, although the author might have built upon a pre-existing folklore to spin this tale. The story involves the three Tamil kingdoms of the ancient era, which were ruled by the Chola, Pandyan and Chera dynasties. Silappadikaram has many references to historical events and personalities, although it has not been accepted as a reliable source of history by many historians because of the inclusion of many exaggerated events and achievements to the ancient Tamil kings.

Story

In the great port city of Poompuhar, on ancient south India's East Coast, Kannagi and Kovalan married. Kovalan saw Madhavi the dancer perform at court, and he went off with her. After approximately one year, Kovalan returned home. He and Kannagi walked to Madurai, a distance of about 250 km, to start a new life. There Kovalan was accused of stealing the local queen's anklet. As punishment, the local king (the Pandian king) put Kovalan to death. Kannagi came to the court and proved that her husband had been innocent of the crime of which he had been accused. She proved her husband's innocence in the following way: She broke open her remaining anklet, and rubies came out (these anklets were tubular, with precious stones inside). The queen's remaining anklet was broken open -- pearls came out. The anklet Kovalan had been trying to sell was broken open, and rubies came out. Thus it was seen that the anklet Kovalan had been trying to sell matched Kannagi's remaining anklet. The Pandian king realised he had done an injustice, and immediately punished himself by simply laying down and dying. Kannagi walked around the city three times, tore off her left breast, threw it against the city wall, and called for Agni, the god of Fire, to burn the city -- but for good people and animals to be able to escape. Agni did as requested. Kannagi wandered westward to the Western Mountains, where some people acclaimed her as a goddess.

Variations in the Story

1. Kannagi was the daughter of the Pandian king. The court astrologer told the king that the king's daughter would be involved with the destruction of Madurai. The king ordered his men to take his infant daughter into the forest and kill her, but instead they took her to the ocean and put her in a basket which they pushed put to sea, and which was eventually plucked out of the water by a fisherman (Beck, 1972, p. 26).
2. The classical text states that Kannagi and Kovalan physically consummated their marriage, and took great joy in each other's loving embrace. An oral version states that they never physically consummated their marriage -- this version seems to treat Kannagi as an unapproachable goddess even at this point in the story (Beck, 1972, p. 25).

3. The classical text states that Kannagi and Kovalan were married for a number of years before they observed Madhavi's dance performance at the Chola king's court in Poompuhar. An oral version states that Kannagi and Kovalan observed Madhavi's dance performance on their wedding night (Beck, 1972, p. 24, 29).
4. Madhavi used a magic potion to attract and keep Kovalan (Beck, 1972, p. 29).
5. Kannagi sent a message to Kovalan, saying that she was dying. It was then that Kovalan returned home (Beck, 1972, p. 24).
6. Kannagi was such a devoted and selfless wife that one time when Kovalan was living at home with Kannagi but was still carrying on his relationship with Madhavi, Kovalan's leg was injured, but he wanted to visit Madhavi anyway. So Kannagi carried Kovalan in a basket on her head so he could meet with Madhavi.
7. Meenakshi, goddess of Madurai, warned Kovalan not try to sell Kannagi's anklet in Madurai (Beck, 1972, p. 31).
8. The Pandian king was hasty to punish Kovalan for stealing his wife's anklet, because he himself (the Pandian king) had been having an affair with a dancer and he wanted to do something to show his wife that he was concerned for her.
9. The court goldsmith in Madurai was in fact the person who had stolen the Pandian queen's anklet. This goldsmith not only accused Kovalan of stealing the Pandian queen's anklet, but also accused Kovalan of having an affair with the Pandian queen (Beck, 1972, p. 28).
10. In Madurai, after Kovalan was beheaded, Kannagi stitched his head back onto his body with a golden thread drawn by a silver needle. Kovalan came back to life. However, as time went on, Kovalan made it clear that he was still in love with Madhavi, and he continued to save the best food (especially mangoes) for Madhavi. As a result, at a certain point Kannagi pulled the thread, and Kovalan's head fell off and he died again. (This episode is narrated by Dr. C. Sumaresan and Dr. A. Ramanathan in the "Episodes in the Countryside" video recording at http://tinyurl.com/Kannagi-Places, beginning at 8:35.)
11. As mentioned, when Kannagi was speaking with the Pandian king, first the Pandian queen's remaining anklet was opened (pearls were found to have been inside); then the anklet Kovalan had been trying to sell was opened (rubies were found to have been inside). Some people say that when Kannagi threw her remaining anklet on the ground -- rubies came flying out, these rubies immediately

burst into flames, and these flames burned Madurai. This version of the story seems to omit Agni's role in and responsibility for burning Madurai -- although it does provide a divine (or magical) beginning of the burning of the city.

12. When Madurai was burning, Kannagi was walking westward. Goddess Meenakshi rushed after her, and pleaded with Kannagi to stop the burning of Madurai. Kannagi finally agreed. This story presents Kannagi as a goddess who at this point was more powerful than goddess Meenakshi. (Please see the video recording at http://tinyurl.com/Kannagi-Places, beginning at 17:40.)
13. There are various claims regarding where Kannagi walked to and settled after she left Madurai. The classical text states she went to Vanci. It is not clear exactly where Vanci was and is. Three other claims (from north to south) are: Valparai (Tamil Nadu), Kodungallur (Kerala), and Thekkadi / Kumili (on the Tamil Nadu / Kerala border). Regarding Valparai, the Mudhuvan tribal people believe: In the time of Kannagi, some of their male ancestors had been advisors to the Pandian king. These advisors told the king, "Kovalan is innocent, do not harm him". However, the king did not follow their counsel. Kannagi requested to Agni that good people should be allowed to escape the fire, so these advisors and their families were able to escape, and they walked with Kannagi towards the Western mountains. They walked to near Valparai, and there in the mountainous forest with Kannagi they founded a new tribe and village. The tribe came to be named as the Mudhuvan people. Mudhuvan people continue today to live in the forest near Valparai.1
14. One oral tradition is that Kannagi was a manifestation of goddess Kali, especially when Madurai was burning (Beck, 1972, p. 28). Another tradition is: After Kannagi had founded a village and tribe in the forest, she was wandering in the forest. Siva came and addressed Kannagi as goddess Shakti. Kannagi remembered her divine nature, returned to her form as Shakti, and ascended to heaven with Siva. This is in the 1941 movie, "Kannagi", by Jupiter Films. In contrast, the classical text states that a divine chariot, in which the resurrected Kovalan was sitting, descended from the sky, Kannagi entered the chariot, and the chariot took them both up to heaven.
15. Following the burning of Madurai, goddess Meenakshi required a number of male members of Madurai's goldsmith community to be put to death on an annual basis, as a collective punishment. After

many years, one man of the community sang so beautifully to the goddess, apologising and asking for forgiveness, that the community was forgiven and the punitive deaths ceased.

Commentary

In Prince Ilango Adigal's classic literary version of the story, Kannagi is a human woman throughout -- except perhaps at the end, when she is taken up to the heavens in a divine chariot with her now divine husband. A number of local folk modifications of and additions to the story present Kannagi as a goddess, or at least an agent of the divine, at various points in the story -- please see above, items 1, 2, 10, 11, 12, and 14. These are examples of the folk's tendency to interpret events in terms of the divine.

Story elements of the Silappadikaram that are variations of themes found in numerous traditional Tamil stories.

Three story elements that are found in the Silappadikaram and also in other Tamil stories are:

1) "A king punishes himself or his family members for misdeeds".
2) "A woman is miraculously served by nature due to her selfless devotion (her chastity) in relation to her husband".
3) "A woman in fury gets justice and becomes a goddess".
    1) *Story element*: "A king punishes himself or his family members for misdeeds". There was a Chola king, Manu Needhi Chola, who had a son. This son was driving his chariot recklessly, and it killed a calf. The mother of this calf, a cow, entered a town, rang the bell of justice (in those days there was a bell of justice near the centre of each town), and told what happened. The king put his son to death as punishment.
    2) *Story element*: "A woman is miraculously served by nature due to her selfless devotion (her chastity) in relation to her husband". Once there was a woman for whom water would form a large ball. She could carry this ball of water directly -- no container was needed. However, one time the woman thought impurely about a man other than her husband, and as a result the ball of water lost its shape and splashed to the ground.
    3) *Story element*: "A woman in fury gets justice and becomes a goddess". This character is very protective of her loved ones -- but if she feels violated, she wreaks tremendous destruction.

Bibliography

Adya Rangacharya, '*The Natyashastra, Eng. Trans: with critical notes*' (New Delhi: Munshi Ram Manoharlal, 1996).

Basham, A. L (1994). Arvind Sharma (ed.). The Little Clay Cart: An English Translation of the Mṛcchakaṭika of Śūdraka, As Adapted for the Stage. Albany: State University of New York Press. ISBN 0791417255

Bharat Gupt, '*Dramatic concepts: Greek and Indian, A study of poetics and Natyashastra*' (New Delhi: D.K. Print world, 1994).

Bracker, Milton (7 June 1953). *"Story of a Determined Lady: Terese Hayden, Sponsor of New Play Series at Theatre de Lys, Is Undaunted Despite Disappointments in the Past"*. New York Times. p. X3.

K.R. Srinivasa Iyengar, '*Drama in Modern India*'.

Kalisada. *Sakuntala.* Translated by Ghulam-Sarwar Yousof. Unpublished Typescript, Penang, 1980.

Oliver, Revilo Pendelton (1938). *Rozelle Parker Johnson; Ernst Krenn (eds.). "Introduction to 'The Little Clay Cart.' " in Illinois Studies in Language and Literature* 23. Urbana: University of Illinois Press. pp. 9–44.

Prema Nand Kumar, "*Indian writing in English*: *Threechee Indian literature*", Vol. XIII, No.4 (Dec, 1970)

"Prof. A. W. Ryder, of Sanskrit Fame; Head of That Department at University of California Dies in Classroom". New York Times. 22 March 1938.

Rajan, Chandra. *Kalidasa: The loom of Time: A Selection of his Plays And Poems*. Trans. Delhi: Penguin Books India Ltd., Print, 1999.

Richmond, Farley P. (1990). *Farley P. Richmond; Darius L. Swann; Phillip B. Zarrilli (eds.). "Characteristics of Sanskrit Theatre and Drama" in Indian Theatre: Traditions of Performance.* Honolulu: University of Hawaii Press. pp. 55–62. *ISBN 0824811909.*

Schallert, Edwin (9 December 1926). *"'Clay-Cart' Hero Wins: 'Twas Ever Thus—Even in the Sanskrit"*. Los Angeles Times. p. A9.

Śūdraka. Revilo Pendelton Oliver; Rozelle Parker Johnson; Ernst Krenn (eds.). *"Mṛcchakaṭikā, The Little Clay Cart: A Drama in Ten Acts*

Attributed to King Sūdraka." in Illinois Studies in Language and Literature 23=1938. Urbana: University of Illinois Press. pp. 45–210.

*The Vikramorvasiyam of Kalidasa.*Trans. Delhi: Motilal Banarsidass Publishers, 1967.

Van Buitenen, J. A. B. *Two Plays of Ancient India*. New York: Columbia University Press, 1968.

Wohlsen, Marcus (2005). *"The Greatest Show on Earth: The First Indian Play Performed at UC Berkeley -- And Anywhere in the United States -- Took the Stage of the Greek Theater in 1907, Along with Elephants, Zebras, and a Cast of Hundreds"*. Illuminations. University of California Berkeley. Archived from *the original* on 16 February 2012. *Retrieved 17 July 2012.*